WHAT PEOPLE ARE SAYING
ABOUT BECOMING FLO

Where did a gender-confused, Orthodox Jewish boy find refuge in the 1920s? In the circus of course. *Becoming FLO*, the eponymous biography of the great Ringling clown, tells the story of the joyful transformation of a sad and abused boy into the gorgeous woman she always knew she was, decked out in flamboyant costumes created either by her or her well-known Hollywood costume designer friend, touring the country as a beloved celebrity at the top of her profession, finally as free as anyone, then or now. *Becoming FLO* is just as much about a little-known, vibrant subculture of cross-dressing, fully out members of the Queer community of gay men, women, and transexuals, who found a home in the circus, which, even more than the theater, was a safe harbor when society wanted them punished and even dead. This story of the remarkable Flo and her colorful world is long overdue and unmistakably cinematic. It deserves a wide audience of readers and viewers alike.

Janet Capron, author *Blue Money*, New York, NY

I read *FLO* with real delight. While I'm sure the story is significant to the author, it's valuable to others and complex in the immigrant/sexuality/profession contexts.

Sian Hunter, senior editor, University Press of Florida, Gainesville, FL

Thank you for writing this…it is an important tale to preserve. I think Flo would like to know that the book…has moved from the reading pile on my nightstand to my research shelves, now sitting between a biography of Mae West and two biographies of Bert Williams…an appropriate arrangement of those four books.

Bruce Johnson, author, former World Clown Association historian, Lynwood, WA

Definitely evocative and special.

George Gibson, executive editor, Grove Atlantic Press, New York, NY

During a time when the Ringling circus advertised "100 Clowns!" it was easy for individual performers to blend into the background. Albert "Flo" White distinguished himself among his peers. His elegant whiteface became iconic among the ranks of circus clowns. We now are given the opportunity to learn the real-life story of the person behind the grease paint. This book is long overdue recognition for a funny man who was also a gentle man.

Greg DeSanto, executive director, International Clown Hall of Fame & Research Center, Baraboo, WI

If ever there were a time to tell Flo's story, it is now. Although Flo was born more than a hundred years ago, this transgender child of immigrant parents who fled religious persecution, this innocent child whose father physically abused her for being an effeminate son, is a symbol of the call for social change and inclusion that is finally in the forefront of the world's consciousness. The courageous young man who fled his father's persecution, joined a circus, and became herself, is an inspiration for everyone who is stigmatized as being "different." Flo shows us how, with an indomitable spirit and generous heart, we too, can disassociate from bigotry, embrace our true selves, and find acceptance and love.

Andrea Markowitz, Ph.D., playwright and author, Phoenix, AZ

I'm thrilled that Flo's story is finally being told. *Becoming FLO* is an important story about finding self-love and the bravery it takes to live your true self, no matter how difficult or how it may look to the outside world. It warmed my heart to see Flo rise up from a loveless and abusive parent to finally embrace herself, inspire and give love to others.

Sharon Preston-Folta, author, book & film, *Little Satchmo, Living in the Shadow of My Father Louis D. Armstrong*, Sarasota, FL

I just finished your beautiful book…what a lovely tribute to a beautiful human. You captured Albert / Flo's essence in these pages. This is also a beautiful love letter to circus life. To me, most importantly, it represents a facet of circus folks whose stories are often untold or quiet. I'm thankful to have "met" Flo.

Aíne Norris, author, circus scholar, professor, doctoral candidate, Richmond, VA

Carson's curiosity led her to research and write *Becoming FLO*, a riveting biography. The book documents her uncle's beginnings, as the black sheep in a family of Russian Orthodox Jews, to his acceptance and embrace from the circus community. He was an outsider welcomed into a family of outsiders. Carson and her siblings loved to hear his tales about the road, about the strange and wonderful people her Uncle Albert encountered with regularity. About the Hollywood circus movies he'd appeared in. Albert White died in 1974, when Carson was 19, but she never forgot

about him, or the stories her grandmother, and her mother, shared when he wasn't
in the room – that he had left home, at the age of 16, to escape an abusive father.
Albert had literally run away to join the circus and never looked back.

Bill DeYoung, author, *Skyway*, journalist, St. Petersburg, FL

If you had attended a circus as a child, *FLO* absolutely will stir up these magical
3-ring memories once filled with adorned animals and colorful clowns. If you enjoy
an excellent underdog story, like flamboyant fashion and titillating travel, real rela-
tionships and faltering families…*FLO*. She may leave you tearful, cheerful, and in
darker places, fearful. A most unique story, this clown fascinates and entertains, as
she did on stage. Joyful and sad, comical and real.

Suzanna Rosa Molino Singleton, author, Baltimore, MD

Carson's uncle was a famous Ringling Bros Barnum & Bailey Circus clown…leading
a double life: one as the man his family knew and adored, and the other as the woman her circus family traveled the country with and accepted for who she was.

Tymber Wolf, Jewish Press, Tampa Bay, FL

What does a 16-year-old do to stop the cycle of unbearable violence in his life once
and for all? He runs away and joins the circus. It was because of the circus that Flo
got to live. A play or a movie, or both, is the natural course that this beautiful story
merits – almost demands. As a descendant of pogrom and holocaust victims and
survivors myself, as well as mother to a 30-something non-binary drag performer,
I can only feel gratitude for those like Flo, who had the courage to find a way to
be who they were in far less tolerant times – making it possible for people like my
child to be who *they* are today – out of the closet, and in public. Thank you, Flo.

**Cindy Stovall, journalist & podcast host, Arts Coast Magazine,
St. Petersburg, FL**

I read the book slowly. It's so emotional, so touching. Beautifully rendered. It is an
act of love through and through, and no reader can miss that. You are so lucky to
have had this man in your life, this uncle, in all his suffering and triumphs. You
write about Flo with so much love and awe…it's very moving. And her family life,
how painful. But she got to live, and that felt like a triumph of love. Religion brings
us together but also pulls us apart, all too often. That Flo kept the photo of her mom
near her really touched me too. It's very special. The photos…add so much. A film!
is what this book requires for sure.

Roberta Israeloff, author, commentator, Scarsdale, NY

I could not put it down! What a fascinating journey and life…I knew him from the many pictures I have seen… but did not know his whole story. I can certainly understand the conflicted feelings he must have had…in an intolerant Orthodox Jewish community and family. It is a wonderful book. The entire circus world should know the story of Flo.

Sandy Weber, board of trustees, International Clown Hall of Fame, Baraboo, WI

I read the book with ease. I like that it was gentle, and that an LGTBQ+ teen could read this and not feel the weight of judgment and shame, but instead the relief if not joy that comes from accepting, respecting, and claiming one's identity. I love this story.

Carol Asch, MSW, social psychologist, Baltimore County Public Schools, Baltimore, MD

Becoming FLO is a triumphant work by a very gifted storyteller. This is an extraordinary true story and a must-read.

Marlowe Moore, author, *Rise of the Freaky Deaks*, Raleigh, NC

Thank you for writing this book. What a wonderful, wonderful person Flo was, and what an interesting way to see how things change over a century for people who are trying to live just who they are.

JoEllen Schilke, host, "Art in Your Ear," WMNF Radio, Tampa, FL

I loved the book. The anecdote from Merle Evans was priceless.

Dan Denton, founder, Sarasota Magazine and CEO, founder, retired at Florida Cities Media LLC, Florida Humanities Board of Trustees, Sarasota, FL

What a wonderful story, Deb. Congratulations!

Raymond Arsenault, Ph.D., author, historian, professor emeritus, University of South Florida, St. Petersburg, FL

BECOMING FLO
...A Mostly True Story

Deb Carson

Pure Art Press

ST. PETERSBURG, FL

Becoming FLO…A Mostly True Story
Deb Carson

Editor: Nanette Wiser
Cover Design: Janet Nummi
Interior Design: Davis Creative Publishing Partners, DavisCreative.com
Photos: Courtesy of Albert White Collection, unless otherwise noted.
2024 Editorial & Design Refresh: Eland Mann, George Stevens

Becoming FLO…A Mostly True Story
Paperback ISBN: 979-8-9911373-0-0
Ebook ISBN: 979-8-9911373-1-7

Published by Pure Art Press
St. Petersburg, FL

Deb Carson performs the multimedia companion piece "The FLO Show," developed in collaboration with creative partner Nanette Wiser. Audiences have proclaimed it a "colorful, lively, joyful and emotion-packed" presentation.

To book "The FLO Show" or an appearance, contact the author at www.DebCarsonWrites.com.

On the Cover:
Promotion photo of Flo/Albert White, Ringling Circus
Courtesy: The Ringling Archives

DEDICATION

Author (left) with sister Sue & Uncle Albert

To Uncle Albert, who inspired me to walk the artist's path;
to Flo, whose creativity and courage inspires us to live life
on our own terms.

FLO—The Meyrowitz Family Tree

Flo's Paternal Great Grandparents: Yakov & Sora

Flo's Paternal Grandparents: Abrah & Bashe

Flo's Parents: Theodore (1868-1930) & Ida Levin (1878—1962)

Flo, Siblings, Nieces & Nephews

Michael (1899 – 1978)

Bertha (1901 – 1931) & Hyman

Rhoda (1902 – 1996) & Gabby

Abraham/Albert/Flo (1903 – 1974)

Elchan "Hank" (1907 – 1995) & Tess

Charles "Chick" (1909 – 1946)

Evelyn (1911 – 1995) & Henry Kallins

Marcia Kallins (1933 –) & Edwin Carson

Debbie Carson, *Becoming FLO* author (1955 –) & Rocky Rinker

Susan Carson Truesdell (1958 –) & Ken Dunaway

Briehan Truesdell (1985 –) & Daniel McElroy

Booker McElroy (2018 –)

Juniper McElroy (2020 –)

Chelsey Truesdell (1988 –) & Jacob Fleisher

Elliott Truesdell Fleisher (2020 –)

Theodora Kallins (1932 – 2001) & Sherwood Platt

Fran Cohen (1952 –) & Bob Heinith

David Cohen (1953 – 2002) & Nancy Eickel

H.J. Platt (1961 –) & Mary Elizabeth Livaudais

Leslie Platt (1963 –) & Dagan Cassale

Emmanuel (1912 – 2002) & Lucille

Florence (1916 – 1997)

Becoming FLO...A Mostly True Story

I recently visited the Ringling Museum of Art's Circus Museum with author Deb Carson in search of photos of her great-uncle Albert White, one of the circus's most acclaimed performers and Ringling clown best known as Flo. I loved Cirque du Soleil, the Big Apple Circus and had attended Ringling's *Greatest Show on Earth* in St. Petersburg and other cities.

But nothing prepared me for walking through the miniature circus set spanning a huge room and with figures created by artist Howard Tibbals, a giant diorama taking you from the circus arrival in town to the backlot of where the performers lived, the animals cavorted and into The Big Top itself. Calliope music, circus ambient sounds and animal cries launched me into Flo's life, and I was instantly transported to a fantastical world.

Becoming FLO...A Mostly True Story author and Florida arts/culture writer Deb Carson captures the roar of the greasepaint and more importantly, the transformation of one young, bullied Orthodox Jewish boy's amazing journey to become Flo in an era of anti-Semitism and homophobia.

As a journalist and colleague, Deb asked me to help her revise her University of South Florida St. Petersburg master's thesis and shape it into an article, book, multimedia performance piece and hopefully documentary after her stint at Eckerd College's prestigious Writers in Paradise conference in January 2020.

I was happy to meet Flo, and although I knew Deb for many years, delighted to discover that she was a talented performer, singer and musician, that her Baltimore family was involved in vaudeville, that her cousin David was a well-known actor/dancer/musician in his youth and that she and David both got the "Flo" gene. Just last week, she unpacked Flo's circus make-up kit while we sorted through photos and illustrations of Flo by master Hollywood costumer Miles White for this book.

Mine Seher Seniye, Ph.D. wrote that Flo's work and life are shining examples. "To me, Flo represents fearlessness, hope and resiliency, a career that stood on diversity and inclusiveness." "It's an important story about a masterful performer and how she thrived within her multiple families, biological and circus-based," writes author and historian James A. Schnur, M.A., M.A.L.I.S.

Alas, the Ringling Circus is no more, and streaming video and other digital delights have replaced the once 1600 performers travelling on four 100-car trains in the 1920s. Even The Big Apple Circus shut down in 2016.

But clowns? Aerial stunts? Until the pandemic, there was an uptick in people taking classes. Rick Wallenda's high-wire walks in St. Petersburg and Nik Wallenda's Sarasota performance still draw crowds and admirers, the last vestige of The Flying Wallendas, friends of Flo's.

For Deb, this book is both an homage to a beloved uncle and a celebration of the "artistic" gene that runs in her family and inspires her life. By writing this book, she uncovers a wealth of lessons and lives well-lived.

Deb's cousin Fran (another Uncle Albert niece), recalls Flo taking her to Venice to visit Karl Wallenda and his family for tea. Says Fran: "I watched Karl's granddaughter Delilah learning to ride standing up on the back of a horse as it ran. When I visited Uncle Albert in Florida, he was often sewing in his room full of sequins, which I love to this day. Another time, we went to a supermarket in Sarasota where he saw an old friend, a tiny little man who had been the coroner in *The Wizard of Oz* and one of the Lollipop Guild kids. I was completely star-struck."

Deb remembers Flo's Christmas parties at his Sarasota home with sister Evelyn, with magnificent spreads of food prepared by both siblings. At Flo's La Tosca trailer park, Deb remembers the stylish parties and Flo showing off a sequined butterfly costume he'd made for a dog act; in fact, Flo was much sought after for uber prop- and costume-making skills.

Deb told me: "To this day, blingy clothes, rhinestones and French cooking remind me of Uncle Albert," who supped like royalty with his sister Jerri and circus pal Kenny at toney Maas Brothers Tea Room and often took Deb and family to Florida fine dining at Pete Reynard's (Anna Maria Island) and The Kapok Tree (Clearwater).

Certainly, Flo lit up both his nieces' and nephews' lives as well as illuminated a path for those who dare dream and defy conformity. Albert White loved being Jewish, being Flo, being her-self, and Deb Carson's book pays tribute to this talented, funny, witty performer and designer.

I think Deb's friend and author Marlowe Moore said it best: "*Becoming FLO* is a triumphant work by a very gifted storyteller. I was hooked on this tale and in love with Flo from the very beginning. Deb has a way of making her uncle our uncle, of making his journey, his hardships, his transition so intimate that I found myself wanting to scream at the other characters, 'it's her, it's her, get out of her way and let her be!' I cheered when she won. I cried when she didn't. This is an extraordinary true story and must-read."

Let me leave you with a circus tradition before you meet Flo. In a July/August 2017 *Smithsonian Magazine* article by Holly Millea, the first and last female Ringling ringmaster Kristen Michelle Wilson said: "We circus people always say we'll see you down the road." I'd like to invite you to travel with young Albert White as he bravely pursues his dream, if not to perform *Madame Butterfly*, but to channel Mae West and other sophisticated ladies in the *Greatest Show on Earth!* as Flo. Enjoy the ride.

—*Nanette Wiser, Editor, March 4, 2021*

Author's Note: Ringling pulled up stakes "for good" in May 2017, but reopened in September 2023, reimagined, sans animals and clowns.

TABLE OF CONTENTS

BECOMING FLO
A MOSTLY TRUE STORY BY DEB CARSON

Author's Note: How Flo Came to Be

In 1903, Abraham Isadore Meyrowitz came into this world the fourth son of an arranged marriage between two Orthodox Jews, Theodore and Ida, who had escaped religious persecution in Russia and emigrated to Baltimore. In addition to Abraham, Theodore and Ida had four boys and four girls. The girls doted on Abraham.

When Abraham was five, Theodore learned the boy had declared to his sister "God made a mistake! I should have been born a girl!" It was from that moment Theodore's rage toward his son began and continued unabated, intensifying over time. For more than a decade, the confused, effeminate Abraham sustained horrific emotional and physical abuse at the hands of his disapproving father. These insufferable conditions brought the young man to a heart-wrenching decision at age 16. Overcoming pure terror and under cover of night, Abraham ran away from home, from his loving mother and siblings, to a life unknown. He would become part of a supportive circus family, change his "too ethnic" name to Albert White, achieve celebrity as a top clown with Ringling's *Greatest Show on Earth!*—and find *her true self*, Flo.

To his sister Evelyn, Albert was her dearest brother. To his mother Ida, he was her dutifully religious, beloved lost son Abraham. To his other sisters, Albert was their idol. To his brothers, he was largely dismissed—until he became famous.

To his father Theodore, Abraham was nothing more than an embarrassment delivering to him regular, merciless beatings. Once Abraham ran from home, Theodore never again saw his son.

To God, she was always Flo.

As for me, Flo was the person I called Uncle Albert until his passing in 1974—and until 2012 when I learned of Flo.

Why write this story?

Most Orthodox Jewish boys at the turn of the twentieth century did not run away from home, join the circus and in this boy's case—find herself. Why indeed. Zora Neale Hurston famously said this about why she wrote her acclaimed book *Their Eyes Were Watching God*: "It was dammed up in me…there is no agony like bearing an untold story inside of you." And so it was with me.

Flo succeeded in overcoming her boyhood agony and lived an incredible life despite all odds. Such a remarkable story deserves to be told. And shared. By doing so, it will perhaps inspire those who seek desperately to overcome their own anguish and live life on their terms. Anti-immigrant sentiments, persecution, hate, intolerance, gender confusion, racism, child abuse and anti-Semitism sadly persist as much today if not more than in Flo's time.

Flo's story shines a light on living a Jewish and LGBTQ life in an era when neither was respected and too often provoked antagonism. During the time of her greatest celebrity, with Ringling from 1949 to 1969, I was curious to know if she was the only Jewish clown among her circus family. I happily discovered a cast of characters who shared her heritage and culture. Not only were Jewish performers some of the country's most famous actors, playwrights, composers and musicians in America during Flo's day, they were also celebrated fellow Ringling clowns.

Jewish circus performers entertained long before and after Flo; many who shared similar ancestral histories including Lou Jacobs, and Paul "Prince Paul" Alpert. Some say Otto Griebling and Felix Adler among other clown greats, were Jewish.

I learned that the Felds, a prominent Jewish family, owned that most celebrated of circuses for longer than the Ringling brothers themselves. From 1967 until 2017, the Felds owned Ringling's *Greatest Show on Earth!* for 50 years until they unfurled the 'tent flaps' for the last time and stored it all away in 2017.

"Jews have a long history in circus extravaganzas. The Moscow Circus, Big Apple Circus, and Cirque du Soleil were all founded or managed by Jews," according to Jewish Studies scholar Dr. Yvette Miller. And like other entertainment industries during that time, stage names regularly replaced birth names to intentionally hide the Jewish identity of circus performers. It was one thing for those behind the scenes to have Jewish names, it was another to have clowns in the spotlight who were thought to be Jews. To list a performer with even a Jewish-sounding name in advertising and programs, would have been detrimental to promotions, resulting in lost ticket sales.

When Abraham Isadore Meyrowitz ran from home to escape his abusive, homophobic father, and joined the circus, he was quickly advised to change his name. Abraham was reborn as Albert White—

the stage name he would become known by as one of the most famous clowns in the world and a Ringling superstar, and the name by which his birth family also came to call him, but who never learned of Flo. It was well into Albert's career that Flo innocently and inadvertently emerged one evening before curtain. When that happened in the 1940s, Albert became forever known by her circus family as Flo, the name she had always secretly called herself.

Flo believed she was a woman born into a man's body, and within her live-and-let live Ringling family, she performed and enjoyed her life as such. Today, Flo would be accepted by most. But in the first 20-plus years of working with smaller circuses, she hid both Flo…and her Jewish identity. Once she joined the Ringling show, Flo fully emerged and performed in exquisitely detailed, feminine clown costumes; notably, she is considered among the first celebrity "drag" clowns.

The legacy left by Jewish and LGBTQ performers like Flo, showcases a bygone world and way of life less accepting than today.

In her signature *Madama Butterfly*-inspired clown whiteface, Flo was one-of-a-kind. A clown and star whose talent in dance, theater and comedy, and her humanity, sparkled as brightly in the center ring, as it did outside of it.

In the end, Flo's unlikely story brims with hope and joy, much like Flo herself. That's what makes it extraordinary, and, I hope, inspirational for those who struggle with persecution, abuse, homophobia and racism.

Deb Carson--March 4, 2021

...Like a Fiddler on the Roof

"Soon I'll be a stranger in a strange new place,
Searching for an old familiar face…"
–from the song "Anetevka," Fiddler on the Roof

In 1830s Russia, the story of Flo's *mishpocheh* (family) is like something straight out of *Fiddler on The Roof*—Jewish traditions, devout families, arranged marriages, and the occasional pogrom. In many ways, their emigration story parallels what Flo will endure three generations later.

When anti-Semitism and turmoil turned Flo's ancestors' lives upside down, they embarked on a terrifying journey from their home, across the Atlantic Ocean to America to escape religious persecution and search for a better life.

Most know of Ellis Island and the welcoming arms of New York City's Statue of Liberty; fewer may know that Baltimore's Locust Point Docks welcomed millions of Jewish emigrants. The early arrivals were Germans. Polish and Russian Jews followed including Flo's family who began their arduous exodus in the 1880s from their home in Kishinev,

Russia. First came Flo's grandfather Abrah with Theodore, who would later bring Theodore's bride (and Flo's mother) Ida.

On arrival in America, immigrants faced multiple obstacles: overcoming language differences, finding housing and earning enough to eat. Often, devout Jews had to forgo—at times betray—their traditions and moral way of life to survive in their new world.

Flo's widower grandfather Abrah had been a successful merchant and a good provider in Kishinev. In Baltimore, he spoke only Yiddish, worked twelve hours daily in a garment sweatshop alongside Theodore, who spoke a little English. Father and son slept on a bare floor in an overcrowded cold-water tenement and shared a sometimes-functioning toilet with five other families. Religious study and worship, *Shabbas* (Sabbath) meals and leisure would have to wait. Time now must be spent working, sleeping and eating enough to sustain them for another day. Theodore often complained. Abrah never did. He and his boy were free. Then and for the rest of his life, Abrah thanked God every morning for awakening in America.

Three generations later, and on the night young Abraham mustered the fortitude and courage to run away from his own persecution, he prayed for his life, an unlikely option had he stayed given his father Theodore's violent abuse. Still, he couldn't know what awaited in the darkness. And like his Russian father and grandfather before him, he prayed it was life. A new and better life.

And it *was* life! And oh what a life it would come to be!

Circus was the most exciting form of entertainment in America at the time, and that is what first attracted Abraham.

Like that of his parents and grandfather, Abraham's journey would not be easy; circus, especially in the early twentieth century, was a hard life. There would be years' worth of dues to pay. Circuses criss-crossed the country in good and bad times, in good and bad weather with little privacy, no bathrooms and few creature comforts.

Clamoring fans saw none of the hardships of circus life, only its excitement and spectacle. When the circus came to town, it was a huge event no matter its size or the size of the city it came to dazzle. Most American circuses started small, rooted in Middle America, but often grew in dimension and prominence. This included Ringling, which was born in Baraboo, Wisconsin, and where today, circus history is still celebrated at the Circus World Museum.

In 1920, C. R. Lamont's Wagon Circus, was the first to provide safe harbor and employment for the frightened runaway Abraham. It was where Abraham Isadore Meyrowitz became Albert White. On he went, honing skills at bigger and better circuses: the Walter L. Main Circus, Russell Brothers Circus, Hagenback-Wallace Circus, Cole Brothers and others until his finely-tuned talents brought the coveted invitation in 1949 to join Ringling Brothers and Barnum & Bailey Circus' *Greatest Show on Earth!* It was also the year Flo came to life.

But her story begins here…

*Hula Girl Flo dances with
clown friend Gene Lewis*

CHAPTER 2

May 1920: The End of His Beginnings

By the second decade of the 20th century, Victorian America was struggling to breathe its last suffocating breath. There was a growing tolerance toward homosexuals, but mostly in places where intellectual life, the performing and literary arts, and bohemian living collided—places like Harlem and Greenwich Village.

Not in Baltimore, and certainly not in the homes of that city's Eastern European immigrant Orthodox Jews whose consultations with their Torah reminded them that men lying with men is an abomination, and that those who engage, or entertain such thoughts, deserve to be killed.

Although 16-year old Abraham wanted to believe and tried mightily to live every day by the age old teachings of his people, his parents and his community, he couldn't stop thinking about the more exciting, glamorous world beyond. Behind closed doors, and away from his parents and brothers, Abraham spoke more and more to his sisters Evelyn and Rhoda about his desires to dance and perform. They had helped Abraham to take ballet lessons in secret.

On a beautiful spring day in 1920, the C. R. Lamont Wagon Circus came to town. When Abraham saw his first circus performance he was thrilled by its spectacle and he liked handsome Christian Pomeroy, a young clown, from the start.

Abraham didn't know that chance meeting would change his life forever. Or that Christian would save his life.

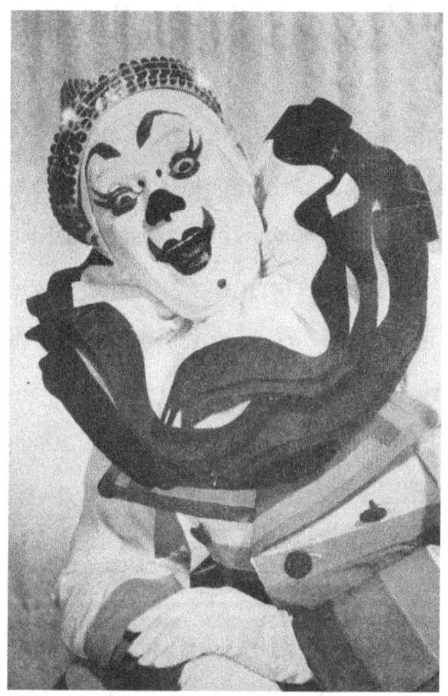

*Flo's storied path led her
beyond her wildest dreams*

CHAPTER 3

May 7, 1920: The Circus Comes To Baltimore

Circus Day in Baltimore, Courtesy The Baltimore Sunpapers

A few days before he met Christian, Abraham had seen the "Circus Day" parade pictures of the Lamont Circus coming into town on the cover of his father's *Baltimore Sun's* Sunday edition. An avid reader, it occurred to Abraham that ever since H. L. Mencken became the *Sun's* Sunday editor, the world opened up to him like it never had before.

In 1920, traveling circuses were a main source of entertainment in small and large towns across America and Circus Day was a huge occasion. Even large cities like Baltimore shut down shops and schools to take in the sprawling display.

As entertaining as it was functional, the parade from the train station to the circus grounds gave gawking fans a preview of the upcoming performance. The circus unloaded colorful railroad cars and walked exotic animals, lively performers and glittering equipment past cheering crowds to where the big top would be erected, a small city unto itself.

Depending on the size of the circus, a Circus Day parade could consist of more than a thousand performers, hundreds of laborers, monkeys, elephants, zebras, lions, gilded wagons, and great billowing tents.

Abraham would awaken early each Sunday so he could be the first to bring the paper to his father Theodore. The stern, unsmiling man expected others to do for him, but rarely appreciated those that did, his wife and children included—and never Abraham.

On this Sunday, Abraham risked sneaking a glimpse of the paper's front page before his father did. He knew if Theodore caught him, there would be hell to pay. There was always hell to pay for something or other Abraham did. And the paper was his father's to look at first, a rule never to be violated…or else.

But Abraham wanted to see the *Sunday Sun's* circus photos so he could weave the images into a dream movie; an imaginary loop where he cast himself as the dancer dressed in a sequined pink costume leading the grand cavalcade.

Today's movie ended with the reality that Abraham would never see a circus. Attending a circus was verboten in the Meyrowitz home. While some neighborhood families relaxed their rules and took their children to the circus, Abraham's family of strict Orthodox Jews viewed circuses as lewd, queer displays of filth and vanity that only "low lifes" as Theodore described them, would associate.

Still, Abraham couldn't help but dream.

At school the next day, luckier friends regaled Abraham with wondrous accounts of the Circus Day parade they attended on Saturday, rendering Abraham unable to concentrate on his studies that afternoon. Knowing Father was in Philadelphia on a sales trip, Abraham rushed home where he excitedly described the vibrant circus spectacle his friends saw as his sisters sat spellbound. Mama Ida smiled and nodded while she stuffed a chicken in the tiny kitchen.

"I wish we could have seen it for ourselves! Mama, do you think we could go to Circus Day the next time one comes to Baltimore?" he pleaded, his lateral lisp more pronounced with each juicy detail, an extreme speech impediment he was mindful to try to control when speaking to his father.

Mama Ida smiled. After 20 years in America, she understood little English and conversed mainly in Yiddish, but understood enough of what Abraham was asking to know her husband Theodore would never allow such an outing. Still, she heard her son's heart cry out.

Following his sisters up to their room, Abraham plopped down at the sewing machine, a happy distraction from circus dreams. He was helping Rhoda redesign her simple dress into a chic frock that would surely win over her dapper new beau.

Abraham's brothers sided with their father and vehemently disapproved of Abraham's interests; his four sisters worshipped him, depending on Abraham for his exquisite taste, kitchen magic, impeccable manners, fashion tips and fine skills with a needle and thread.

With Theodore not expected home for hours, the three siblings were certain they would be safe from their father's iron fist today.

Theodore left early that morning to travel the two hours north to Philadelphia for his work with Butler Brothers. He failed to close a big sale. One of the haberdashery's most successful salesmen who started as a tailor, Theodore had worked at Butler Brothers for years, the premiere men's clothing stores for Baltimore's wealthiest Jews and prominent country club set.

No one heard Theodore's key turn the front door lock. The darker the man's mood, the stealthier he moved. He was home early. Steeped for hours in a murky temperament since abruptly leaving Philadelphia, his fury bubbled just below the surface, barely held in check. Theodore was primed for evil.

He entered his home and closed the door behind him, turning swiftly to ascend the stairs to his room. Theodore slowed only long enough to heave his hat and coat over the banister toward his startled wife, glare at her and through gritted teeth seethed *"UNDISTURBED!"*

Reaching the top of the stairs, Theodore howled when he caught sight of Abraham at his sisters' sewing machine. "Enough!" he raged. Screaming incoherently, he dragged his son by his hair from behind the sewing machine. Digging his fingernails deep into Abraham's scalp, he hurled the boy across the hard floor. Abraham's body stopped when his head hit the cold iron radiator—face first.

In the commotion, the heavy black sewing machine toppled to the floor and banged its way toward Evelyn, missing her by inches. With his black belt doing the talking, Theodore delivered his second beating to Abraham in a month; the worst and most violent than all the rest.

Ida stood frozen in fear, horrified by what she heard upstairs. She was often horrified by her husband's behavior, but as always, felt it was not her place as a dutiful, obedient wife and observant Jew to cross Theodore.

And yet, this explosion crossed a line.

She ran to Abraham and helped him to his bed. His color mimicked that of his white bedsheets save for the bruising and blood. Ida implored Theodore to take Abraham to the hospital. He slammed the bedroom door in her face. Ida returned to her terrified boy to clean his wounds and tender a mother's balm. Eventually, Abraham fell asleep.

As the household quieted, Ida busied herself. She cleared the table of Theodore's untouched, cold congealing meal, tidied the kitchen, then sat for a long time staring out beyond the back screen door into the clear night sky. She reasoned that as an observant Jew and obedient wife, God also expected her to be a good mother, one who protected her children. Ida prayed for guidance.

***

As dawn came, abandoning all hope of sleep, she began to prepare the tea. As the kettle rattled and a small stream of steam escaped, it came to her.

"I *am* a good mother," she firmly reminded herself, "I shall take Abraham and the girls to the circus Friday afternoon after school."

She realized it was a grave risk not consulting her husband; she surprised herself by her uncharacteristic boldness choosing to defy him. "I hate what this man is doing to my son," she quietly spoke aloud, scowling and raising her hand that involuntarily clenched into a tiny fist. "This will help Abraham forget his bruises and lift his spirits. Theodore be damned! God forgive me."

Jews believed at the time, "If you talked of a terrible sickness, it would come to you." Theodore's 'terrible sickness,' his abusive behavior toward his family, but especially Abraham, remained a secret. And the family's silence was expected.

Neither did Abraham speak of it thereafter, or ever, but for different reasons. He swore this incident would be the last he would endure from anyone, his father—most of all!

***

The C. R. Lamont Wagon Circus was a small circus compared to Ringling, but no less exciting for a big-hearted beautiful boy with a battered soul like Abraham.

Struck by the sheer joy the experience brought to Abraham, Ida consented to his request to go backstage after the show. He wanted to meet performers and have them autograph his cherished program. Despite Ida's limited understanding of English, she looked at the program in his outstretched hand, sized up his wide-eyed, piteous black-and-blue expression, and agreed.

Seeing how jubilant this made Abraham, the girls cunningly persuaded Mama Ida to take them after the show for Lime Rickeys. The concession stand that served the tasty tart beverage was in the opposite direction from where Abraham was headed, and thus the girls concluded, this would give their brother ample time to visit with the performers without having to hurry. Everyone agreed to meet back at the circus entrance in an hour and head home.

The dazzling sights and unforgettable smells were riveting! Abraham approached the tent where he first saw Christian—a tall, wispy feather of a boy, leaning rakishly against a pole. His long, clean red hair, smattering of freckles and turned-up nose complemented his creamy fair skin. Abraham had never seen such a boy!

Christian was alone. His fuchsia and purple costume contrasted with the rest of him, especially his alabaster face—which held traces of clown white the washcloth missed. Abraham held out his program to Christian, whose infectious smile lit the space and faces of both boys.

Introducing himself with a flourish, Christian signed Abraham's program, a trinket he prized for a lifetime. Abraham could hardly take his eyes off Christian, but finally found his voice and asked the intriguing young clown how he came to join the circus. To Abraham, the captivating Christian was from a different world but seemed only slightly older than himself.

"Well sir, I was born in Lumpkin County, Georgia, where a few generations back, mah 'kin' went a lookin' for gold. Them Pomeroys? They was dirt poor, sharecroppers living on next ta nuthin' in West Virginny. They heard about a kinda Southern East Coast gold rush there in Georgia, so pulled up stakes and just a' went. They never found no gold, or much else. Even after I come along, some three generations later, there was still nothing," the unassuming boy added.

And because there was nothing for him, Christian explained, he left home three years ago to join the circus "the very first time it come thru where we was living." This last piece of information from Christian especially piqued Abraham's interest.

Lamont Circus

Christian went on to describe his impoverished family, their failed farm with never enough to eat and too many mouths to feed. At midstory, Christian noticed Abraham's shiner for the first time but didn't let on and continued in a voice that bespoke of empathy—and what Abraham realized later, solidarity.

"Before he left Ma and me, Pa would take to the bottle, then to us—quite regler. Ma said ta go. It weren't right to leave her, so I stayed. Leastways for awhile. One somebody had to look after her and that was me. Plus, where was I gonna go? One night it got real bad. Before the next sun, Ma and me left for her sister's place way up north—to Illinois. Alton. Alton, Illinois. If Pa lived or died, we still don't know. Don't care."

Abraham grimaced. What Christian described felt a little too close to home. Pushing it from his mind, Abraham turned to the more electrifying topic of how Christian came to be a part of this exciting life—the circus!

"Ok, well, when Ma first started a tellin' me I should leave, I started askin' ma'self, 'wellsir, where wouldja wanna go, Christian?' I remembered hearin' stories 'bout the free and easy life of ridin' the rails like so many other kids from the Midwest was a doin'. At first that seemed real excitin'. Who wouldn't wanna ride on them big ole trains and see the world? But then, it started to seem less appealin' thinking how cold 'n dirty it'd prolly be." Abraham hung on every word. "No dough to boot, 'lessen you boosted it from some other poor kid. And that wuddena been right. We was used to poor, but I didn't wanna be no hobo. One night, after we was a livin' up Alton way, I heard tell of this circus group whose winter quarters—I didn't know what that meant then—whose winter quarters was in Alton, and that they'd be a' comin' back real soon."

"Now circus—circus seemed real excitin'—the costumes, the travelin', the trains. Yessir. I'd never been ta no circus, but I heard tell of 'em and saw some pixtures once't in a magazine. Come ta find out that 'winter quarters' is the home place for where a circus sets when it come off the road -- and that was Alton! Wellsir, as soon as them circus people got ta town, I started hangin' 'round The C. R. Lamont Wagon Circus' winter quarters!"

"Oh, we have 'em now, as you can see, but back then, they didn't have no trains…just wagons, but they was surely the most colorful 'n carved woody wagons, trimmed all in gold, not real gold—only paint ya see, carryin' all sortsa animals 'n the funniest lookin' people I never knew lived and breathed in these here U-Nited States of America."

"There was this thing called the Midway, kinda the 'before-show' on the way into the big top, see? There was half men/half women, bearded ladies, snake charmers, midgets, even a two-headed tattooed boy! It was, it was…well, downright fer-eign is what it was, I tell you! And pretty darn excitin' ta boot!"

Abraham was spellbound by this charming stranger with his dancing eyes and enticing, simple ways. Sensing Abraham's "green light" reaction, Christian continued with renewed vigor.

"Then come the animals, mostly biguns from Africa and such—a elephant, zebras—they're like horses with stripes, monkeys…all sorts, a lion and the shiniest horses—the reglar kind—I ever did see. You could almost see your face in their shine! Them horses had pink feathers they'd wear like little hats on their heads! Our Midway is smaller now, and the main show is kinda big now, as you prolly saw today, but we still have lotsa them funny people and animals."

"But the clowns—they was my favorite. Still are. No matter how low ya felt, they'd raise yer spirits. If'n ya felt pretty good to start, they'd lift ya even higher. They were like one big family—and they're so happy. You cain't help but wanna be aparta a family like that. So I worked real hard to become one—a clown, ya see? And I did. Imagine, bein' happy and having fun! All the dang time. And gettin' to wear all them colorful, satiny and sparkly costumes. All the dang time! Ya know, once you're inside them clown costumes, you can be anybody ya wanna be. And— get this—clowns all wear special clown makeup, see. And, once a clown creates his own special face—and they haveta on accounta them bein' a clown there is this unwritten rule, a clown law that says nobody can ever copy yer face. And nobody does! It's a matter of trust…and honor and…respect!"

All his life, he had been taught that trust, honor and respect were hallmarks of a proper Jewish life. But in Abraham's Orthodox Jewish home, the practice of these tenets all too often fell short.

Abraham found in Christian a kindred spirit and perhaps, because Christian was so different, Abraham might dare share secrets with Christian who listened with his whole soul.

While a thousand thoughts ceaselessly circled inside Abraham's head, Christian quietly sized up his new friend's face, waited, then spoke again, gently and plainly.

"Come with us," he said.

Lightly brushing the purple on Abraham's bruised cheek with delicate fingers, Christian reached for Abraham's hand and looked directly into his eyes. "Sure, a lotta us here have run away from somethin', but dontcha see? We've run to somethin' too, somethin' good. We're a family. We look out for one another. We're safe here."

Abraham looked away. Christian paused, then brightly, "We have fun, we travel, we even make a little dough. And see, we get ta wear a lotta different kindsa costumes. And hey, look! We can help each other design our own clown faces! I haven't pur-fected mine yet, and I bet you'd be real good at helpin' me—and creatin' a bang-up one for yourself!"

A minute passed. To Christian, it felt like an eternity and again he searched Abraham's face. When Abraham looked up, his eyes sparkled and his smile broadened into a wide grin. This time it was Abraham who reached for Christian's hand. It was as if the door that Abraham thought would be forever closed, was opening; a feeling that transcended all pain. It felt magical. And it felt right.

The circus would be leaving town soon, Christian told Abraham, and if he wanted to join them, he would personally see to it that Abraham would find a happy, better home.

"The train leaves at midnight on Sunday. The tents will be down, but the ticket booth will be up—them roustabouts haul it onta the train last. Be there by 11 p.m. sharp…'ll be a waitin' for ya, Abraham." Christian pulled a worn bandana from his back pocket. "You'll recognize me by this here red scarf. I'll have it tied round ma neck."

Abraham savored the moment. Even the smell of circus was intoxicating as he walked slowly back to meet his family, replaying Christian's words, considering countless possibilities. By the time he reached Mama and the girls, Abraham was convinced of what he would do. Must do. Rejoining his mother and sisters, they couldn't help but see the glee on Abraham's face. It had been gone for so long. He tried reigning in his emotions, but his eyes betrayed—they were afire!

Abraham nattered on nonstop about the people and sights behind the scenes, but mostly about Christian. He proudly showed off his program now sporting Christian's signature purple-inked autograph but was careful to reveal nothing of his epiphany.

Nearing home and retreating further and further from the circus and Christian, Abraham's resolve waned. The sun was descending, and with it, darkness began squeezing out the light which, less than an hour ago, illuminated Abraham's soul.

"It would be easy to leave Father; he would probably like nothing better," Abraham bitterly thought as his fingers found his painful, bruised face. "But what of the girls? Of Mama? Graduation? Will Father turn the whole family against me? How could I live with that? What about money?

Warm clothes? Enough to eat? What if I got sick who would take care of me? Could I return home—ever?" The walk home turned excruciating and exhausting.

Abraham thought he was keeping his racing emotions hidden by continuing to chat happily about the great day. Evelyn sensed something else. She said nothing to the others; she would talk with her brother in private. Later.

Once certain most were asleep, Evelyn appeared. Abraham could read his sister as masterfully as she could her brother. Without a word, they tiptoed down to the parlor and sat close. He would tell her.

Abraham confided everything to Evelyn. She listened to his desires and his fears, and candidly voiced her own. They talked until there were no more words to say. Dawn came, and with it, the realization that neither could deny. Pulling her brother close, Evelyn whispered in a voice of desperation. "You must go." They both knew Abraham had to extricate himself from this life or fade away forever. A ghost.

The next night, Saturday, Abraham revealed the details of his plan with Evelyn, who on this night he called 'Rivvie,' his pet name for her, derived from her Jewish name Rivka, "servant of God." Strong like Mama's mother Yetta, Evelyn would not fall apart. Unlike Yetta, Rivvie listened. Tonight, he needed someone to listen.

"If only I'd been born a girl, Rivvie," Abraham cried, "I'd never have to go." He feared for himself, but also for his sisters. And for Mama who was about to give birth to her tenth child at age 39. Theodore kept Ida pregnant for most of her married life and she was so exhausted. She lost a baby last year, distraught after Theodore beat Abraham nearly unconscious. Would his running away cause Mama to lose this baby?

Abraham spent Sunday on tenterhooks. As evening arrived, the darkening sky crept like molasses toward midnight. Abraham knew it was tonight or never. This wasn't the first time Abraham thought of leaving, but the first time he would go.

From under his pillow Abraham pulled Mama's lace handkerchief and wiped away the remaining tears, mindful of his still tender cheek. Mechanically, Abraham emerged from under the warm covers, swung his legs over the bedside, stood upright, and smoothed the rumpled clothes he'd slept in.

Feeling like he was sleepwalking through a nightmare, the powerful instinct to turn back gripped every cell. He closed his eyes and the memories flooded back in. He opened his eyes. Rage replaced fear; he moved now with purpose.

Maneuvering deftly around his sleeping brothers, he took one surreptitious glance before moving on to the girls where he addressed each. "Mazel tov, Bertha," eldest and soon to be married; next four-year old Florence, the youngest who adored her brother, "I adore you too little beauty." Next, elegant Rhoda, "Thank you for your grace and kindness," and finally Rivka, to whom he now trusted his life, "God keep you safe." She awoke, and their eyes briefly held one another.

Passing his sleeping parents, Abraham froze as his gaze fell on Mama's face; the untimely upwelling of sorrow, love and guilt almost caused him to turn back again. Right then, his father stirred, and instinctively, Abraham fled.

He slowed enough to creep down the worn creaky steps that led to the kitchen, turned the knob opening the back door, soundlessly closed it behind him and inhaled the dank night air that met him on the back stoop. Some spectral force drove him onto the cracked asphalt alley that disappeared into the beyond, still feeling the kiss Evelyn left on his baby-smooth forehead hours ago, the warmth of her arms which voiced her 'goodbye.'

Snatched rudely from that memory when some night creature skittered closely by, Abraham's menacing thoughts swiftly returned; his shoes feeling cemented to the ground below him. He squeezed close his eyes, took another long breath and prayed—first for the family he was leaving behind, not knowing if he would again see his mother or sisters, and second, for himself. Once more, the invisible power began gently prodding him forward.

Steeling himself against the years of unrelenting terror now behind him, but with the unknown ahead, new tears threatened. For a third time, Abraham dug deep. Recovering his courage, he pressed on. He pulled his jacket and knapsack around him a little tighter, turned up his collar against the night and gaining momentum, disappeared into the late spring drizzle.

He thought now only of Christian.

"Please God, please let Christian be there waiting for me like he promised." The desperate prayer swirled in Abraham's head, growing louder with each mile that widened the distance between what could only be—no, MUST now be, his former life.

"Oh God, too much time has passed! Is it past 11?" He knew it wasn't, but Abraham was so anxious. The unrelenting chorus behind his eyes was joined by the booming thump thump thump in his chest. "Oh God! I've walked in the wrong direction!"

Panicked and about to give in to his worst fears, the dissonance abruptly halted when the scent floating on the night air entered Abraham's nose and consciousness. It quieted him, and gently urged him on.

The strengthening aroma was something not altogether unpleasant, and somehow familiar. All at once he recognized the perfume that could be created only from the mixture of elephants, sawdust and roasted peanuts! He stopped. In that moment, the whole world stopped.

Abraham inhaled the wondrous scent. The smile that started down in his soul now played across his lips. "Thank you, God" he murmured.

His heart was pounding, now with anticipation. In the distance, a large tent was still standing; he saw its silhouette from the light that lit it from inside. A delighted squeal escaped from deep within Abraham. It was the Big Top! And there he was! The red neck scarf. It was Christian!

1920–1926: First of May

"braham, yer what they call a 'Firsta May.'" Abraham's head tilted. Christian repeated the phrase, speaking more slowly, at a lower pitch and enunciating each word. "A Feeeeersttt offfff Mmmmaaaaay." It's what circus folk call first-timers who ain't never worked ina circus. A Firsta May. That's what you are, Abraham! It's real special. And yull be cut some slack on accounta everybody knows who's new cause they just come on with us." Abraham nodded.

"Now, first things first," Christian's tone changed. "I don't mean no disrespect, Abraham, but no one, but no one will hire somebody when his name sounds so uh, um…fer-eign. I seen it already once't before."

His birth name, all three pieces of it—Abraham Isadore Meyrowitz—branded him as one who had come straight from his ancestors' *schtetl*, which, arguably, he had. Abraham received Christian's meaning loud and clear.

Flo's early days as a clown

"Besides," said Christian taking a chance and hoping to interject some humor into an awkward conversation, "everyone would be a lookin' for yer horns!" Both boys dissolved in laughter but recognized the seriousness of the situation. Abraham had come this far. He couldn't risk not being hired and certainly not because of a name that could be so easily changed. Following Christian's wise and worldly counsel, Abraham would be reborn with a new name, his 'stage name'—"Albert White."

Christian introduced Albert White to Charles Lamont, and after a brief audition, Albert was welcomed into the C. R. Lamont Wagon Circus family!

Now with a proper—and most unquestionably unquestionable moniker firmly in place, Albert White followed quickly in Christian's footsteps, starting his circus career as a hawker just outside the entry to the circus grounds, and in sight behind him, the entrance to the Midway. Albert enthusiastically enticed folks to "Hurry, Hurry! Step Right Up….!"

In his former life, *schmaying*, with his sisters had been among Albert's favorite pastimes. Now, after each show, Albert would entertain Christian with stories of the many excursions he and his sisters took into downtown Baltimore for window-shopping and adventure. Soon, Christian began to regularly ask in his own, special, multi-syllabic southern Yiddishe-speak, "Say, Albert. What time do ya wanna go a' scha-my-in'?"

Albert eagerly awaited the same question he knew would come each day from Christian. Like all such moments reserved only for best friends, Albert never tired of hearing Christian's question; Christian never tired of asking so he could hear Albert's distinctive lispy cackle one more time.

Several happy months passed with Albert adding new skills and friends by the day. One afternoon, Charles Lamont asked him to substitute that evening for Bernice, the show's Bearded Lady. Bernice had fallen ill the night before. Sad to hear about his friend's illness, Albert was elated to get his first opportunity to work inside the Midway—and as a woman to boot (albeit a very hirsute woman).

With only hours to spare, Albert went to work preparing a proper act including costume, props and makeup. Truthfully, he had prepared for just such an opportunity. In his first performance as a bearded lady, he quickly proved that his hairy character could also be funny, delicate and a lithe dancer.

Because of Albert's act, Bernice's old stage was becoming one of the Midway's most popular sideshows. Lamont rewarded Albert by making him the new permanent Bearded Lady. Bernice was angry at first, but even she couldn't deny Albert his due. She moved on to share a stage where she created a new act with Tiny, the smallest and most talented of all the midgets. Bernice's character, Half Man/Half Woman, and Tiny began drawing crowds of their own.

Christian was proud of his friend; Albert's terrific gig was credited with drawing sizeable crowds to the Midway and the Big Top. But as much as Albert loved his new role and appreciative audiences, he felt like a captive after just a few weeks.

As a hawker, he and Christian could quickly change out of their costumes, go into town and explore after each show. But as the Bearded Lady working the Midway, Albert couldn't be seen inside the show or about town as anything but THE Bearded Lady. Such was the case with all the "freaks" who performed on the Midway.

As much as Albert disliked feeling like a hostage, he came to realize, "Who would ever again pay to see a live two-headed baby, a half man/half woman or a bearded lady if they were not real!"

The price of the Midway's pretense hit home when Albert had to miss a performance of *La Bohème* in Cincinnati. Christian had never seen Albert so upset. That lisp was out in full force, as was "Baby Rose" whom Albert inserted into conversations when he was overwrought, talking to familiars, or his secret self.

"Uh, uh, uh, Baby Rose, I am no prisoner!" Albert clucked. It may not have been Albert's treasured *Madama Butterfly*, nonetheless, he was missing his Puccini! Albert consoled himself by quietly humming "Un bel dì vedremo" the most famous aria in the great opus. Suddenly, the solution to his Bearded Lady conundrum came to him, as if it was a gift delivered from Cio Cio San herself!

The next day, Albert had breakfast with Bernice. Drawing her out as only Albert could, Bernice finally admitted she missed her beard. "It makes me feel safe, Albert. I feel so exposed having to be a half of a woman and a half of a man—neither have beards!" Albert looked straight into Bernice's sad eyes, patted her hand sympathetically and said, "I've got something I think will cheer you up." He told Bernice he had created a clever new Bearded Lady routine, that he wanted Bernice to have it, and give her back her old job. "I can teach it to you right away. And Bernice dear, I'm certain it will be an act Mr. Lamont will adore." Albert knew how much the boss liked his Bearded Lady's dancing. Generously, he incorporated some deft new moves for Bernice to use.

"Well, what's there for you to do Albert?" asked Bernice. Albert answered, trying not to sound as excited as he was. "Well, I've developed another character for myself—as a hawker again, but with a twist. We can do a lot more with costumes and routines to get people to buy more tickets," he confided. "The act I've created for this character will really spice things up outside the gate. I'm sure Mr. Lamont will find the idea and increased tickets sales irresistible."

And he did! Lamont was pleased with both new acts, just as Albert promised. Albert made everyone happy. He liked doing that.

Thinking back, Albert realized his secret ballet training in Baltimore before he left home last year had, indeed, come in handy. Albert's all-new character was quite exotic. Lamont loved exotic and Albert knew it. Lamont gave it his gold seal of approval. With meticulously applied geisha-inspired makeup a la 'Cio Cio-San', and slipping into the colorful, silken costume he had fashioned with his own hands, Albert shape-shifted as a striking Asian dancer.

To keep things fresh, Albert prepared yet a second character, a pretty hula-dancing Hawaiian girl. Many thought Albert silly to give up the Midway, considered a better job by most, and return as a lowly hawker. Albert wanted to prove how hawkers could be more creative and successfully drive ticket sales when they were entertaining and colorfully costumed, not dreary and dirty.

Albert told Christian: "Hawkers are the first thing you see at the circus—they are the face of the circus! There should be all-excitement and allure out front!"

The worst hawkers were the barkers who wore stained clothing, stank of stale beer, and dangled shaggy old stogies from sickly mouths that croaked out tired, old solicitations.

"Hurry, hurry, hurry! Step right up and…" …'Run away!' concluded Albert, who replaced their repellant unclean, uninspired demeaner and tired invitations with clever words, colorful and crisply laundered get-ups and lively actions soon after his first weeks with Lamont. Albert jazzed up the humble hawker's job further by adding intricate choreography and amusing props. In no time, Albert's changes at the Lamont Circus entrance were a big hit and moneymaker. His captivating characters enticed prospective audiences with tantalizing free previews of what the Midway and Big Top entertainment provided once people bought their tickets. So successful were Albert's Geisha and the Hawaiian Dancer performances that Charles Lamont added stands at three more cities extending the season by several weeks.

In costume, no one thought Albert was anything other than a woman; such was his style, grace and elegant movements. Despite Lamont's addition of more hula dancers, all female, Albert stood out as the best and most beautiful hula girl. With so many supportive circus friends and the popularity of his two engaging feminine gags, Albert finally began to relax in his skin among his unique new family.

He wrote regularly of all this to Evelyn in the clandestine letters he mailed to the post office box she set up just before her brother left home. Albert was overjoyed when he found Evelyn's note with instructions and the address zipped into the pocket of Michael's jacket—the one Albert wore the night he left home. Thankfully, Evelyn didn't have to wait long for Albert's first letter which helped soothe the frayed nerves of his anxious sisters and mother.

In July, Evelyn wrote that Mama had given birth to a stillborn male. Albert was riddled with guilt. Evelyn told him the midwife said the baby had not developed properly and was doomed from conception, assuring him that his departure had nothing to do with the miscarriage. Still, Albert was inconsolable knowing the grief and suffering he no doubt caused Mama—about which he could do nothing. Evelyn encouraged her brother to write regularly about his new life. Albert's newsy and amusing letters help lift everyone's spirits, especially Mama's.

For the next ten years, Albert wrote every day keeping his sisters and mother up to date on his life as a circus performer, his new friends, and his travels to places his family could only dream of visiting through his missives.

Theodore never knew of his son's letters to his wife or daughters. Nor did he ever ask if they had heard what became of his son. Perhaps he didn't want to know. Or he knew and didn't care. Or considered his son dead.

On the Lamont show, Albert's work as a clever, beautifully costumed hawker soon moved him past the entrance, beyond the Midway, and into clowning and the show's center ring. Albert kept Flo closeted inside, but in the spotlight, she shone. Christian and his fellow clowns were thrilled for their friend's success.

On the Lamont show, Albert and Christian were never far apart. Despite coming from such different worlds, they brought out the best in one another. In fact, they were inseparable, their friendship had grown deep roots. Working and living side by side, the boys spent all their time after shows and in the off-season exploring cities and towns across America during its Roaring Twenties.

By 1926, Albert was ready to test his clowning mettle in a bigger ring, so when the offer came from the Walter L. Main show, he was packed and ready. That Christian had left a few months before, made Albert's decision to leave much easier. He was sad and somewhat lost without his trusted friend. Christian told Albert that he wanted, no needed, to go back to Alton to be with his terminally sick mama in her last days. He had been sending money home to his mother for the last two years. "I gotta go Albert. I need ta hold her in my arms once't more in this life."

It was useless to hold back tears. Christian shouted over his shoulder as he boarded the train, "I'll be back ta ya real soon, Al-bert!" Albert heard the lump that caught in Christian's throat, and was reminded of another painful parting—his own six years before.

Willing himself to feel nothing more than the evening's cool breeze, Albert stood on the platform trying to make out the caboose as it became one with the horizon, "*Zay ge'zunt*," was Albert's prayer and farewell to Christian.

1926-1930: The Gatsby Era

America was in a partying mood, willing to spend money on all kinds of entertainment. Multiple circuses criss-crossed the country, vying to be bigger, more ambitious and awe-inspiring than their competitors.

Albert kept making new friends, inspiring audiences and surprising himself. His gags, costumes, props and face became more intricate and sophisticated, and his popularity soared. More confident in his talent, he dreamed about joining the world's grandest, most prestigious and wealthiest circus—Ringling. And continued keeping Flo in check.

In 1927, John, the last surviving Ringling brother, had accumulated so much wealth that he relocated the massive production's winter quarters from Wisconsin to sunny and warm Sarasota, Florida. Ringling had recently built an extravagant Venetian Gothic mansion on the town's picture-perfect turquoise bayfront he named Ca' d'Zan.

Albert stayed with the Walter L. Main Circus for three years before moving up to the Russell Brothers Circus in 1929, until America's party came to a screeching halt when the stock market crashed, and the Great Depression sunk fortunes. Some circuses consolidated or were purchased by larger ones; many folded. Albert's employer at that time, Russell Brothers, hung on by a thread.

It would be a whirlwind few years for Albert, navigating his professional clowning trajectory from circus to circus, advancing what would become lifelong friendships among new circus families all along the way. As for Albert's biological family, the regularly sent and received letters to and from his sisters and Mama Ida were a lifeline, but everyone's deepest hope remained that they'd reunite someday, knowing that couldn't happen as long as Theodore was alive.

Ten full years and a lifetime from when a terrified boy left home in order to live, daring to hope too for a better life, cancer took Theodore's life. The news caused Albert to want to leave immediately for Baltimore, but he would have to wait a little longer before he could return home to the family he'd left so long ago.

It was 1930, and the Great Depression had wreaked havoc on the ability for multitudes of businesses to survive, including circuses. Still with Russell Brothers, Albert learned that the show would close its season four months early. Many performers abandoned the show before it officially ended its run, but Albert was loyal. He'd given his word to management to work to the season's end, whenever it came.

Albert had lived each day of those ten years on the road with the deep-seated anxiety of never knowing if he'd ever see his birth family again. With Theodore gone, he ached to go home. But he had made a promise to his employer, and dutifully waited. Performing now for half empty houses and listening to the sorrow in the voices of his fellow performers who stayed on but had no place to go when the season did end; the wait was more arduous. From the day he learned his father was dead, Albert counted the days, the minutes, until he could board a train for Baltimore.

That day finally came, and the reunion was jubilant; better than he'd imagined! Albert's sisters were so grown up. Bertha, named for their kind-hearted Russian grandmother Bashe who died in childbirth—and Albert's oldest sister who married the winter after he left home, was living in Baltimore. After years of trying, she and her husband were soon expecting their first child.

Rhoda too, had married, and made her home in Huntington, West Virginia. The couple was childless and would remain so. Her husband worked for the B & O Railroad so it cost Rhoda nothing to take the train home and stay with Bertha and her husband, which she did regularly.

Evelyn had recently married as well and lived in Baltimore. To be nearest to Mama during his long-awaited visit, Albert stayed with her. Ida lived with her son, Albert's oldest bachelor brother Michael and their baby sister Florence, who was a spinster but not by choice. Neither Michael nor Florence had married—and never were to marry. They were coerced to remain single, and live with and care for Mama Ida until her death which wouldn't come for another 32 years in 1962. Theodore had commanded this sad arrangement for his oldest and youngest two children. Included in Theodore's will was the stipulation that noncompliance would result in the two heirs being cut from any inheritance. In death, Theodore was as vile as he was in life.

Nonetheless, everyone was thrilled that Albert was finally home! All the siblings who weren't already living in Baltimore made sure to visit as often as their schedules allowed during Albert's stay. After having acclimated to and enjoying being constantly on the move for so long,

Albert surprised himself with how content he felt to be off the road. He was finally in the arms of his loved ones after so very, very long, overjoyed to be able to spend long hours with each of his sisters, especially their families whom he had come to know only through letters.

On the first Friday night *Shabbas*, Albert escorted out every sister who tried to help him in the kitchen. This was Mama's kitchen, but even she was turned away. That evening, the best chef couldn't have topped the savory chicken francais with lemon tarragon Albert served on Mama Ida's good china. The fancy Greek potatoes with feta and gingered carrots were simply out of this world! Everyone said so.

Exposed to places, cultures and people from across the globe, Albert's culinary repertoire held many dishes none of the Meyrowitz' had ever heard of, much less sampled. When the Persian cinnamon pistachio babka was brought to the table still warm and served with butter adorned by paper-thin slices of red pear, the entire table *kvelled* with delight!

After dinner, Albert brought out Grandmother Yetta's silver service—one of the only treasures she secreted out of Russia to America hidden in the layers of her clothing. Serving freshly brewed coffee and chocolate non-pareilles to his loved ones, Albert felt a sense of belonging and happiness that had eluded him growing up.

Days with the family catching up often melted into evenings. A lot of laughter and love, so long overdue, was shared generously. But after a month, the road called. This time, so different from the last, Albert left knowing that no matter where he was in the world, he would always be with family—either his circus family or now, again, his Baltimore family! Still, Flo remained tucked safely out of view.

1931–1945: The Great Depression, WWII & Chick

A few months prior to the stock market crash, John Ringling had purchased the American Circus Corporation, a conglomerate which operated six circuses, including the highly regarded Hagenback-Wallace Circus.

Albert had begun performing with Hagenback-Wallace in 1931 and was thrilled to be under the Ringling umbrella of circuses, closer to his dream. His star continued to rise for the next seven years until early 1938, when a bigger circus came calling. A Ringling rival, Cole Brothers reached out to Albert. Former clown mates working now for the Cole Brothers show, soft-spoken Kenny Dodd among them, had recommended Albert. A protégé who held great respect for one he considered a gifted mentor and friend, Kenny wanted the best for Albert. Cole Brothers was playing Memphis, a few hours by train from Hagenback-Wallace's current stand in Tupelo, and Kenny took the opportunity to visit Albert for a few days.

Albert had been doing well with Hagenback-Wallace, and reasoned it was a solid stepping-stone to Ringling. "Kenny, best that I turn down the Cole Brothers offer, at least for now." Kenny paused, then gingerly pulled the ace from under his sleeve. "Albert, we both know Cole Brothers is a great show and a Ringling rival in many respects. We're drawing huge crowds, some as big as Ringling's, even bigger since they brought on Clyde Beatty. John Ringling wishes *he* had Beatty– along with those 30 roaring lions of his!"

Kenny paused. He let that bell ring. He knew Albert recognized it was a great offer—more money, more spotlight, bigger audiences. He also knew Albert could be stubborn. "Albert," pressed Kenny, "take the offer. You'll do well with the Cole show, and eventually get your Ringling invitation. When that time comes, and it will, you'll be better positioned to leverage what you've done for Cole and get Ringling to better its offer—money perhaps, surely more time in the spotlight."

An ambitious dreamer and one of the best, most creative clowns of the era, Albert was also a practical businessperson. "Kenny may be right. I could do more in the bigger arena under better lights." Such was Albert's last thought before sleep came that night.

Over breakfast he told Kenny, "Ok, Baby Rose, I'll do it!" After submitting his heartfelt resignation letter and having shared tearful goodbyes, Albert left with Kenny for the Cole Brothers' show. It was a good move. A very good move. Hagenback-Wallace pulled up tent stakes for good once the season ended.

Flo's clown pal Kenny Dodd

After living under all those silks, sequins and sizzle for many years, and now with a new show, Flo was more restless than ever. Despite Albert's fear of revealing his truest inner self, regardless of the closet in which he tried keeping her tightly locked, Flo was beginning to tiptoe out.

Albert's success with Cole Brothers blossomed, and with it, a new-found confidence in himself took root. More closeted than even Flo, confidence and trust were stunted early in his life, beaten out of him by his father. Now that real celebrity was before him, friendships established and time-tested over two decades, Albert began letting down his guard ever-so slightly, and slowly.

Trust was something he almost allowed himself with Christian—they were together day and night for nearly seven years. Albert was as vulnerable with Christian as he'd been with anyone. In some ways, even more so than with Evelyn. On more than a few occasions, Flo nearly escaped. But when Albert and Christian parted ways, Flo remained inside. Christian instinctively knew of Flo, absolutely. It was the boy's innate grace that he chose never to mention her to Albert. Christian believed it was simply enough to know she existed; it was unimportant to Christian to know her by name. She was right there, in front of Christian every day. He loved her.

Many more perks and freedoms were enjoyed by Albert with Cole Brothers—better costumes, more privacy on trains, more time in the center ring. He was asked to produce a few acts with fellow clowns, and all became hugely popular.

Best of all, Albert had more time off between some of the Mid-Atlantic stands allowing him quick visits to his Baltimore family. And after his first two years with Cole Brothers, Albert could finally return to a real home off the road at the end of the season with his dearest sister Evelyn in Baltimore and her precious little daughters.

Evelyn's husband Henry, a truck driver, regularly accepted long hauls which kept him away for extended periods. Their girls, Marcia and Theodora, one more adorable than the other, loved having their Uncle Albert home. He doted on them. Just like he did with his own sisters growing up, Albert helped his nieces learn to cook fancy dishes, shop for new frocks and make up their faces—sometimes as clowns, sometimes as movie stars! Being able to come home to Baltimore was a blessing for everyone.

Sadly, the eldest Meyrowitz sister Bertha died in childbirth, repeating the same fate her grandmother Bashe, for whom she was named, suffered so many years ago. The tragedy multiplied when Bertha's widower Hyman asked to marry the youngest Meyrowitz sister Florence. Although everyone agreed the new baby needed a mother, and Florence thought she could learn to love Hyman, the marriage was verboten. Florence and the eldest Meyrowitz son Michael were still living with and caring for their aging mother Ida, as decreed by Theodore's will. Michael remained vehemently opposed to losing the inheritance. "No" came Michael's flat answer to Hyman's plea to marry Florence and have a mother for his infant girl. "No, impossible," Michael repeated.

Florence's life was beset by troubles, *tzuris* as the family's Yiddishe-speak described it. She was never the same after this setback. Florence had survived childhood polio and later, a broken engagement to a wonderful boy whom she loved and who Theodore banished, and now this. Albert knew his baby sister's spirit was broken forever. From that moment on, he vowed to become her protector.

Florence never managed to dig herself out of her depression, but the country did. Soon, Albert was back on tour for his next dazzling season with Cole Brothers. Circuses were thriving again, as was certainly the case with Cole Brothers. Albert was a happier and busier performer than ever before.

Into Albert's mounting circus success and his family's reunification came a sad episode with his brother Charles, whom everyone called Chick. Growing up, Chick was despised by his father almost as much as Theodore despised Albert. Perhaps Chick would have lived a different life had he too run away, but he didn't.

From birth, Chick seemed emotionally unstable. His mental health issues were exacerbated by the physical and emotional abuse he too suffered at his father's hands. Chick was always in trouble. Stopping at the corner store one afternoon on his way home from Hebrew school, two policeman found Chick stealing a candy bar and brought him home. Theodore took the incident as his opportunity to send Chick away to St. Mary's Industrial School for Boys, a home for wayward youth. By the time Albert ran away from home, Chick was 11 and had spent a year at St. Mary's where young Babe Ruth lived down the hall at the cloistered school with the terrifyingly dark reputation.

Chick lived there until he turned 17, aging out with nowhere to go. He had no desire to return home. He knew Theodore had long dismissed him as "dead"; Chick returned the sentiment. Living on the streets of West Baltimore, Chick panhandled and drank in gritty bars. In a drunken haze during a lost weekend, he and a wizened prostitute from a neighboring barstool got married; it lasted a week. The woman left town with whatever Chick had in his pockets, never to be seen again.

Evelyn, the self-appointed family caretaker told her brother, "Chick, you will move in with us so you can get sober and back on your feet." Always soused and stinking, his pint bottle of cheap scotch peeking from his filthy back pocket, Chick quickly landed back on the street.

Before the serious drinking began one evening, Chick passed a storefront; its windows were plastered with patriotic posters. He stumbled in and signed up to join the Army. He told the recruiter that he wanted to do everything to help America defeat the Japs and the Krauts. No one else wanted him, but Uncle Sam did. Off he went to boot camp, then on to North Africa where the fighting was fierce. His family could only pray for his safety.

During an evening performance in Denver, Albert in the wings awaiting his cue, he received a telegram from Evelyn. Chick had been taken prisoner. Albert was barely able to perform. He didn't really know Chick, yet always felt sorry for him for the abuse and terror Theodore wrought upon his delinquent brother. Albert was still Chick's flesh and blood. From her note, Albert knew Evelyn was distraught. Muddling through the subsequent days and weeks, and sustained little by updates from Evelyn, Albert tried to call his sister and mother from the road as often as he could. His voice, which took all his strength to calm before he dialed, soothed his sister and mother, he knew.

Chick, a POW for two years, was physically tortured, and exposed to chemical weapons. When WWII ended, Chick was released and sent home to Evelyn. It was evident he would not live long. For a second time, Evelyn desperately tried to care for Chick but realized quickly her labor of love was impossible. She agreed to move Chick to the nearest VA neuro-psychiatric unit, which was in Delaware. Chick barely survived two weeks before his sad life ended when he succumbed to his massive injuries.

The funeral was held without Albert who wasn't able to take the time off; it was the busiest part of the season. Finally approved for leave that would get him to Baltimore a month after Chick died, Albert ached miserably concluding he wasn't strong enough to face the sadness and memories that Chick's tragic life and death triggered. During times like this, it helped Albert to think of his circus family as his real family, who, in such situations understood him better than his sisters and brothers.

Flo caught in the act as she prepares for the show

Flo prior to her Ringling years

CHAPTER 7

1946–1949: Hello, Flo

Albert was spending more time in the center ring, more confident and comfortable in his skin. Lately, he had developed some new and significant friendships with fellow clowns that led to a watershed moment in his life—the emergence of Flo.

Flo had been inside Albert for so long, that when it happened, Albert wasn't prepared when Flo innocently sprang to life.

The matinee curtain was due to rise in 20 minutes. Albert pulled his chair close to the edge of his dressing table, taking one last long look at his makeup and costume in the oversized mirror when Flo slipped out. "Oh honey, the sequins on that hat look like dreck. You can't wear that hat looking like that, oh, no you cannot Miss Flo. No, no, no, Baby Rose," he murmured to his reflection, staring at the tiny hat's ornamentation and tilt.

Albert had found a delightful and deepening friendship with "Blinko," so named because of his signature two and a half inches long, sparkly green eyelashes that glittered against his clown's white face when he blinked. His real name was Ernie Burch. Albert liked him immediately. Liked those eyelashes too. Just the night before, Albert had confided to longtime clown friend Jackie LeClaire what he thought of Ernie, "Oh those looong eyelashes! A very nice touch, oh yes indeedy! That Ernie Burch is soooo handsome, so sumptuous with those gorgeous smoky eyes against velvety skin and all that dark ruffle of hair under his wig and gold hat!"

Nattering on now about his own little hat to his mirrored reflection, Albert was unaware that Ernie was in the dressing room; that anyone was there. So meticulous was Albert about his look, he'd long ago earned a deserved reputation for being last to leave the dressing room. Hearing Albert, Ernie wondered "who is Flo? He's talking to someone named …Flo." Ernie

Flo's friend Ernie Burch

was curious, but didn't want to impolitely interrupt the conversation, so quietly stepped around the partition, stopped by where Albert sat, but saw no one else. Startled, Albert stopped talking when he realized Ernie was behind him, then squealed in horror, mortified realizing that Ernie probably heard Flo.

Albert nervously busied himself, pulling tissue after tissue from the Kleenex box on the dressing table, pretending—praying Ernie hadn't heard a word. Unconsciously, delicately dabbing at his décolletage with one of the tissues that hadn't floated to the floor, then fanning himself with what remained of the one in his other hand, Albert noticed Ernie was smiling, his big emerald lashes dancing.

A playful guy at heart, Ernie impishly asked, "Albert, who were you just talking to?" Ernie liked Albert too. "Oh, honey, I was just talking to myself about this wretched little hat. I've tried but I can't do a thing with it. The sequins don't catch the light well, and the colors are all wrong, and…"

Flummoxed, Albert interrupted himself and stopped speaking. His pronounced speech impediment was out of control and had become quite juicy. The tissues were a godsend.

Smiling that disarming smile of his, Ernie placed his warm hands on Albert's shoulders and with quiet intent, spoke. "You were talking with someone named Flo. Who's Flo?"

Like it or not, Flo was out. Flo stopped dabbing and nearly stopped breathing. She forced herself to settle and quickly considered her options. The voice in Flo's head spoke and it soothed her. "Flo honey, Ernie will understand." Flo took a deep breath and the risk. They had a few minutes before curtain.

"Well, you see, Ernie, I've always thought of myself as Flo, and always called myself Flo. I've been doing this for as long as I can remember. It feels better when I think of myself as Flo. A woman."

Ernie started to chuckle, and for a moment, Flo flashed on a very dark childhood memory. Her stomach churned, convinced she had made a huge mistake. Ernie sensed this and quickly pulled over a chair, placing it behind Flo, and sat. Ernie bent forward and good-naturedly placed his head next to Flo's, balanced just so on her shoulder.

Smiling, speaking to Flo's reflection, Ernie calmly and evenly said, "So from now on it should be—and shall be Flo. That's who you are, inside and out, and it suits you perfectly."

Flo was stunned. Again her stomach fluttered. A very long moment passed between them, then relief. Relief beyond belief! Flo was suddenly swept back to her time with Christian. She had almost shared her secret with that dear boy years ago, but the time hadn't been quite right. It was now with Ernie.

Flo fought the urge, mindful of her perfect face, but lost. The tears came. After all these years, someone finally understood! Ernie pulled the remaining tissues from the box and handed them to Flo. It was a new beginning, and the start of what would become a deep friendship, one that nurtured the next chapter of Flo's life and success.

As a child, Flo wanted to understand. She had wanted desperately for her family to provide answers that never came. Questions weren't allowed to be asked, and when they were, they brought extreme emotional pain and violent physical suffering. Abraham and Albert were exhausted having fought anguish and shame for so long. It was Ernie's tender coaxing that liberated Flo. She loved him for it.

From that day forward, she was forever known by Ernie, and soon thereafter by all her circus family as Flo. But only to her circus family. To her fans, she remained Albert White; to her Baltimore family, Albert.

CHAPTER 8

1949: The Invitation – Ringling & Fame

In 1949 all of Flo's hard work, all the travel, all the joy would come to be amplified a thousand times over.

Cole Brothers was playing an engagement in Peoria and Flo was waiting in the wings for the evening show's finale to begin. Just before she heard her music, someone from the front office came running down the backstage ramp. Breathless and nearly knocking into Flo, an obtuse young man in an ill-fitting brown shirt, brown vest and brown pants held out an envelope. Flo was annoyed by the boy's

Ernie Burch and Flo—Ringling era

clumsiness and putrid nicotine-smell, not to mention being so rudely interrupted moments before stepping onstage.

Flo plucked the envelope from the boy's offending yellow fingers, glad to be wearing her clown gloves, and carefully placed it deep within her oversized bodice in that place where her "falsies" and bra ended, and her costume began. She made a mental note to immediately launder her gloves and undergarments as soon as she got back to the train.

Extricating the envelope from her bodice, its mystery getting the better of her, Flo quickly scanned a group of nearby showgirls and asked the one in the tall, feathered headdress, but no gloves, to please tear open her envelope. Flo thought she looked the cleanest of those gathered. Flo began reading—and froze. She almost missed her cue. The telegram inside was from Mr. Pat Valdo.

Pat Valdo joined Ringling Brothers in 1902 and by the 1920s, had become one of the circus world's most prominent whiteface clowns. John Ringling thought highly of Valdo as a performer, but also saw in him, a man who had the respect of almost everyone on the show—from all his fellow performers—equestrians to side show freaks, aerialists to clowns, the bandmaster and the ringmaster, but also laborers and animal wranglers, cookhouse staffers to advance men, ticket takers to the big money managers. Ringling soon recognized he could leverage Pat Valdo's broad talents beyond those as a performer.

By the time John Ringling moved the show's Winter Quarters to Sarasota from Wisconsin in 1927, Valdo had already been promoted to the executive position he would hold with the *Greatest Show on Earth!* for the next sixty-plus years.

As Ringling's Director of Performance and Director of Performing Personnel and its chief talent scout, there wasn't a circus performer alive who didn't know who Pat Valdo was. Or wanted more than anything to receive THE invitation from him.

Flo achieved her lifelong dream of performing with Ringling, finally earning the most coveted invitation she could have ever hoped for—a clown alley spot with the world-famous Ringling Brothers and Barnum & Bailey's *Greatest Show on Earth!*

"Oh indeed I am, honey! Miss Flo is now in the highest of clover, Baby Rose!" Ringling was the world's largest, most celebrated circus of all time, and it showcased the most prestigious clowning troupe ever. When there were more than five thousand professional circus clowns working in North America, Flo became a member of Ringling's Clown Alley elite during that circus' golden years. There, she lived and worked with Emmet Kelly, Felix Adler, Jackie LeClaire, Lou Jacobs, Otto Greibling, Prince Paul, Frankie Saluto, and Gene Lewis among others, all of whom enjoyed lifelong friendships with Flo.

Ernie "Blinko" Burch, to whom Flo innocently revealed herself during their time with Cole Brothers, was already performing with Ringling in 1949 having received Mr. Valdo's coveted invitation a few months before. So Flo was thrilled that she and Ernie would be travelling together to Havana, Cuba to perform for the first time with Ringling! What a debut! And with Ernie. Life couldn't possibly get any better. By joining Ringling, Flo was home, a star among stars.

The night she left the Cole Brothers show and boarded the train to join Ringling, Flo did what she did every night. She prayed and gave thanks to God for her life, wonderful families, and abundant good fortune. Laying in her berth, Flo gazed at the picture of Mama Ida on the wall beside her and said "*A gute nakht, Mamaleh.* Good night, my little Mama. We had a good show today. *Shlof ge'zunt.* Sleep well."

Flo couldn't have known how famous she would become with Ringling: photographed by the famous Weegee outside Madison Square Garden, wearing and designing costumes for herself with the Broadway

Tony-winner & Hollywood Oscar-nominated Miles White, appearing in Cecile B. DeMille's Academy Award-winning film *The Greatest Show on Earth!*, serving as Martha Raye's double in the film *Jumbo*, featured on the cover of the *Baltimore Sun's* "Sunday Magazine," and so much more. Flo's life with Ringling exceeded her wildest dreams.

Havana, Cuba

Flo, Ernie supping with Ringling clown friends and crew in Havana

It all began when Flo joined Ringling on December 8, 1949 as part of a new month-long holiday show in Cuba, a first for Ringling. Opening night was a huge hit with one *New York Times'* reviewer writing "Havana went wild over the performances and gave Ringling's *Greatest Show on Earth!* the warmest reception it ever accorded a visiting amusement organization."

Just as Havana embraced its first major circus, so too did the Ringling troupers take to the 'Gay Paree of the Caribbean.' Touring lively Havana, they enjoyed the colorful city's freedoms and its exciting diversions for all types and tastes.

On the morning of the opening show, Cubanos headed for work or play dressed perhaps more gaily than usual—the circus was in town! "Imagine," Flo murmured to Ernie as they prepared to leave their hotel to explore downtown Havana, "we are finally here! And we're together in this vibrant city. We're in a country only 90 miles from America, but a world away from anything or any place we've ever known. Well, certainly none that *I've* known." Days before, Flo had confided to Ernie why her abusive father led her finally to run away from home. Ernie caught Flo's dark meaning and quickly turned the moment to light. Smiling that dazzling Ernie smile—the one that animated his face from ear to ear, he brought Flo close and whispered "Flo, you are lovely. I can't wait to show you off."

Handsome olive-skinned Ernie could have been mistaken for a Cuban native, dapper in his crisp white guayabera, perfectly pressed tan linen trousers and sporting a Panama hat.

For the first time ever, Flo dared to appear in public as her true self in this magical place. The trousers and shirt she had always worn off-circus grounds as a shield, remained neatly folded in tissue paper in her suitcase. On this day, she floated to Ernie's side in her gossamer, peacock-hued frock that matched a stunning pair of expensive slippers she'd indulged in at her favorite boutique, LongtallSally's in Chicago. Flo loved pretty footwear and wore it regularly inside her big clown shoes, a secret little *amuse bouche* only she knew (or so she thought).

Today was different. On this morning, the new cerulean blue peau de soie slippers would be on full public display, sparkling with tiny sapphire glass beads Flo had painstakingly applied.

Moving through the streets to the rhythms of this sultry, frangipani-scented otherworld, Ernie and Flo promenaded arm in arm down the famous Paseo del Prado to the shimmering harbor, hopelessly intoxicated by this sun-drenched city and one another.

Ernie and Flo were dazzled by the attention of the locals, despite the fact that neither understood a word of Spanish. "Ernie, we're not yet on stage, and look at how we're being received by these beautiful people! Even the young ones are pointing, laughing and clapping their hands as we walk by! They probably know we're part of the circus and are cheering us as performers and Americans! Just listen," Flo whispered.

The couple returned huge smiles and enthusiastic waves as everyone they passed gleefully shouted, '*Maricón!*' '*Maricón!*' '*Maricón!*'

Still floating on air, in dramatic fashion later that evening in the dressing room, Flo regaled her fellow clowns of the couple's glorious reception. It was later that Ernie learned '*Maricón*' did not translate to 'American'—but was instead the crude Spanish slang word that translated as 'faggot.' No one had the heart to tell Flo the truth that day—or ever.

For Flo, Havana's tropical fairytale morning shared intimately with soulmate Ernie remained a treasured, long-held memory. Over the years, Flo would often gather new and old friends, and share her Havana story again, as only she could, innocent of the slurs she mistook for admiring words.

The Famous Hollywood Costume Designer

Flo had already won over multitudes of circus fans and circus family before the end of her first full season with Ringling. Among them was the renowned stage and screen costume designer Miles White who had been chosen as costume designer for Cecil B. DeMille's epic film *The Greatest*

Show on Earth! White was traveling with Ringling to soak in every aspect of circus before filming was to start.

Shooting in Sarasota began in 1951 during Winter Quarter rehearsals. Flo appeared in numerous scenes. After the film's huge success, in large measure because of his costuming, Miles White stayed on with Ringling for several seasons as the circus' costume designer.

A handsome bon vivant with a captivating personality, Miles' looks were a little bit Cole Porter, a little bit Oscar Wilde. His talent and wry sense of humor further attracted the effervescent Flo…and he was smitten with her as well.

From the first, a bond was forged between Miles and Flo when they discovered they'd both chosen White as their respective stage surnames. Miles was simply mad for Flo and created magnificent works of art that became Flo's show-stopping clown wardrobe for many tours in the 1950s and into the 1960s. Miles also loved a good prank!

True to its acronym, circus 'Specs' are indeed spectacular.

Flo in Miles White costume

Intent on stimulating every sense, the Spec is like a dazzling Broadway overture in that it primes an audience's proverbial pump for what's to come. The Spec opens each show with a prodigious parade around the outer track where props, animals and performers in their finest, circle all three rings, inside of which, lesser action is simultaneously happening.

The Ringling Spec was the grand entry set to big orchestrations, meant to show off circus in all its glory, and often revealed that season's theme. Acts and costumes were often created as subthemes like "The Wild West," "Carnival in Venezuela" and "The Coronation of Mother Goose."

The coveted spot for the Spec's lead "payoff" float is traditionally meant to seat *only* the show's most beautiful woman who sits high above all the action. More than once, Miles snuck Flo atop the payoff float.

The first time was in 1956; the theme "The Coronation of Mother Goose."

Perched proudly on her first payoff float, Flo played the role of the newly crowned Mother Goose regally waving to her 10,000 adoring fans from on high. "Flo would positively glow when we pulled our little capers. And she always kept me out of trouble by carrying the part off like the grand diva she knew in her heart she was," quipped Miles.

Miles was tickled by Flo's considerable collection of magnificent size 11 designer slippers, and one of a few friends to whom Flo eventually confided that she wore them inside her clown shoes. They were her pride and joy.

In 1957 before the show at Madison Square Garden, a new boy, lost and hastily trying to find his way out from the clowns' dressing room, stepped on a new fancy pair of Flo's slippers she thought she'd safely tucked out of sight under her makeup table. "Flo screamed like a banshee at the unfortunate boy, 'Watch what you're doing you clumsy bitch!' It was so far out of character for Flo, that for one fleeting moment, everyone went silent," Miles recalled. "A beat later, the room exploded in laughter, led by Flo's own guffaws. Once she caught her breath, she sincerely apologized to the poor wide-eyed lad, and then to the room at large. I'll never forget that moment. Or Flo."

La Tosca -The Turquoise Temple

Flo's distinctively painted home in Sarasota's La Tosca Trailer Park was the site for her frequent, fabled parties. Sarasota was sprinkled with many such parks where Ringling performers and staff called home from the 1930s to the '60s. A December tradition, Sarasota's resident and visiting families would eagerly await their annual holiday car-ride through competing parks after sunset to ooh and ahhh at glittering light displays and cast their votes for "Most Festive Christmas Park." With Flo directing the project for La Tosca's holiday entry, it was no wonder that park reigned supreme and held the winning title for more than a few of the near-ten years she lived there.

Flo bought her turquoise temple in 1950 at the end of her first season with Ringling. There, she was surrounded by her closest circus family members. It was the place she could finally call her own since escaping the terror of her Baltimore home 30 years before. La Tosca was known as the park with the liveliest residents and parties. It was the perfect locale

Flo/Uncle Albert at home

for Flo to settle into and enjoy life when she and her circus family were off the road.

Miles White loved visiting Flo at what he christened and was forever known as "La Tosca's Turquoise Temple." Besides being a world-famous costume designer, White was known to friends as a well-seasoned, world-travelling gent.

With a twinkle in his eye meant especially for Flo, he liked to tell the uninitiated, "When I'm relaxing in Flo's trailer, I feel as if I am in the most luxurious, well appointed, French whorehouse."

"It is THE place for Flo's potato pancakes…all of us gather there for those delicious morsels!" Fellow clown Kenny Dodd would smack his lips as he greeted guests new to one of Flo's famous Sunday brunches.

Flo generously treated her most appreciative diners to gourmet meals fit for a French king. Kenny was among her regulars, and Flo was always grateful that he convinced her to leave Hagenback-Wallace and accept the invitation to join him on the Cole Brothers show a few years before they both joined Ringling.

Another La Tosca visitor and dinner regular was the endlessly talented and irreverent Jackie LeClaire, whom Flo met early in her Ringling career. Jackie was second-generation-circus, a great conversationalist and storyteller, eternally armed with hilarious stories to share.

Jackie was born on a Ringling backlot in the 1920s to circus-performer parents. He grew up and was educated away from the sawdust. Reaching adulthood and returning to Ringling, Jackie worked primarily as a clown but followed in his father's footsteps and began his Ringling career as a flyer before moving to clowning. In the mid-1940s, Jackie was temporarily pressed back into service posing as a female flyer, subbing for his injured friend Greta. Flying too closely over a group of rowdy sailors who jeered and cat-called to Jackie realizing he wasn't a woman; Jackie was grateful for Greta's return the following week.

In 1951 when *The Greatest Show on Earth!* was filming, and because of Jackie's abilities as a flyer, Jackie was once again asked to "fly." On this occasion, he was thrilled to have been selected as the stand-in for lead actor Cornell Wilde whose character, The Great Sebastian, was a flyer. Jackie's ample trapeze talents are on full

Flo with elephant and 2 friends

display in a lengthy and pivotal dramatic segment in the film.

In 1960, Flo's ten-year residency at her La Tosca Turquoise Temple came to an end when she learned her sister Evelyn and former brother-in-law Henry were remarrying after their divorce that had lasted five years. Recommending a fresh start, Flo convinced the newlyweds to move from Baltimore to Sarasota. At the end of Flo's 1959 season, the threesome pooled their money, purchased and moved into a tidy 2-bedroom/1 bath, terrazzo'd floor ranch home within a mile of La Tosca.

Homes in La Tosca were often passed down within circus families. And so it was with Flo when she sold the infamous Turquoise Temple to clown friend Gene Lewis. Gene later sold it to Jackie LeClaire. By the late 1960s when Jackie moved out, Kenny Dodd proudly proclaimed ownership of the Turquoise Temple. He would be the home's final, happy resident until the park, like many others, was sold to developers who built tidy ranch homes, much like the one in which Flo, Evelyn and Henry lived.

Flo's most famous promotional glossy

CHAPTER 9

1961: A Brief Departure Blows Flo's Cover

Ringling may have made performers famous, but not prosperous. Flo was granted a temporary leave from Ringling in 1961 for a better paying but mind-numbing commercial gig as Richo the Clown, the mascot for The Rich Plan Frozen Food Company. As Richo, Flo accompanied their star salesman to sell freezers and frozen foods to housewives and their hubbies across America.

Flo's decent but strait-laced traveling partner —and bunk mate— was salesman Walter Howe, who knew not of Flo, only Albert. Within the first two weeks of the new gig, Flo knew she'd made a mistake. The money wasn't worth the drudgery nor was the Herculean effort it took to re-closet her true identity.

She soldiered through a soul-sucking, sunless sales tour in western Pennsylvania and New York for the first three months of her year-long contract. One dreary morning, Flo's spirits lifted when she realized she and Walter would be in Utica at the same time as Ringling. She missed her friends terribly, and her life with them. In her excitement, Flo thought it would be a cordial gesture to invite Walter to meet her Ringling friends and treat him to the show. She was pleased that Walter quickly accepted. Then reality set in.

"I can't retract the invitation, that would be so declasse! Jesus Christ! Oh shit. What did you do Baby Rose? None of our friends are Walter's er, cup of tea. Oh, my my my Jeeee-susss Chrrristtt, what have I done?"

Flo could not afford to have her Ringling family risk blowing her cover with Walter. She devised a plan.

Flo dressed in her most lackluster man-clothes, mirroring Walter's own, benign beige-on-beige attire. On the way to the arena, she constantly reminded herself to act like the Albert that Walter knew, no matter what. They arrived at the stage door and once inside, Albert signaled to Walter that he needed the rest room, and for Walter to stay put. He did.

Mouth agape, Walter was immediately distracted by what he was seeing. Only three feet from where Flo left him, an elephant and her handler in matching hot pink tutus stood, awaiting their cues. Seconds before, Flo had bolted, making a beeline for the dressing room.

Although she hadn't seen her friends for months, Flo entered and uncharacteristically, came right to the point. She cautioned everyone about Walter. "HE, Walter, DOESN'T know and should NEVER know OF or ABOUT FLO!"

After a breath, she continued, pleading, juicy lisp flying, "*PLEASE un-der-stand!* Walter Howe is a nice man but doesn't know *an-y-thing* about me. NOTHING!" She raised one eyebrow for effect. "So whatever you do, DON'T call me FLO. Do ya hear? Don't call me FLO! For *heaven* sake, DON'T CALL ME FLO! To Walter, I am Albert. Call me Albert. AL-BERT!"

From within the dressing room, everyone recognized the tip-off that meant the show was set to start in 20 minutes. They heard the orchestra, conducted by the incomparable Merle Evans, rehearsing the first few bars from Bizet's rousing overture to *Carmen*. As he had been doing for Ringling since 1919, Evans typically conducted 200 pieces of music per performance, and never once missed a show. Evans was a Ringling fixture, respected worldwide and loved by all.

Satisfied she'd thoroughly forewarned her fellow clowns, making each swear to safeguard her true identity, Flo breathed a sigh of relief. She left to retrieve Walter and escort him back to the dressing room to meet her friends, where after the brief interlude, she would usher Walter out so they could blessedly take their seats.

Flo led Walter back through the door from which she'd just exited, and down the stairs into the dressing room where she cheerfully greeted her friends as if she hadn't seen them in months. Excitedly, she introduced Walter to each. "Oh hello Albert, how are you…?" "Oh, yes, good, yes, thanks, and this is my friend Walter Howe, the salesman I work with…" Polite repartee continued as calm poured over Flo, confident that things were going as she'd hoped.

No one noticed the music had stopped. No one noticed that Merle Evans now stood at the landing atop the stairs leading into the dressing room. Merle hadn't known that Flo was expected that day. He lit up when he spied her in the crowd below. With his bigger-than-life booming baritone voice which needed no microphone, Merle bellowed "JESUS CHRIST, JEEE-SUS CHRRRRISSSSTTTT, IT'S FLO!

Flo froze, feeling the train wreck unfold before her. Any other time, she would have been overjoyed to see Evans, but shaken to her core by his greeting, she stood paralyzed. A Shakespearean range of emotions played across her face in one split second. Stuttering and stammering, she managed only to sputter "Oh, oh, oh my…" before she flew from the dressing room and ducked into the nearest rest room she could find. Of course, it was the ladies rest room.

Flo was eternally grateful to Jackie LeClaire who finished out her Richo the Clown contract so she could return home to Ringling. She resolved to never again act as anyone other than herself.

Flo, happy among her Ringling family again

CHAPTER 10

1962–1967: Lessons Learned

Flo was elated to be home in Sarasota, reunited and working with all her Ringling pals. For all her friends had done for her during and after the ill-fated Richo boondoggle, she wanted to do something special for them, something that would make their life easier.

Many were parents, and those that weren't found themselves pressed into service when it was less than convenient. Flo and the circus offspring were a match made in heaven; Flo's loving care and time was a welcome gift to everyone, including the children!

Flo knew she could offer much more than babysit, and so created "Flo's School of Fun." She created a plan, set a date and distributed colorful flyers meant to entice children and parents.

The day before school was to open, seven children had signed up. "Okay, okay, more than I was expecting. Oh Jesus Christ, SEVEN little ones…oh shit…" Flo thought of recruiting help. She worried she was over her head and for a minute, considered ditching the idea, then admonished herself for considering such a thing.

She wagged a finger in the air. "No, no, no Baby Rose. YOU are no Indian Giver. No ma'am. No Indian Giver. You can do this! For chrissakes

Flo, how many babies did you help raise? How many children have you entertained and delighted? That's right. Thousands. THOUSANDS! That's right now, Miss Flo. This will be easy—like cake on a spoon! Tomorrow, come hell or high water, honey, we begin!"

Flo and the sun rose early; it was going to be hot. Looking for something cool to wear so no sweat marks would show, she selected a lightweight white tee shirt complemented by airy plaid shorts and her everyday tan thongs. She applied three layers

Flo inspiring young artists

of Mum Extra-Strength cream deodorant, finished dressing, dabbed a splash of Chanel here and there, and rolled the cart she'd completed filling with supplies the night before to the patch of grass she staked out previously, and posted a colorful, sparkly "Flo's School of Fun" sign she'd created in the shade of a big tree.

On this quiet spot, Flo placed a small table surrounded by ten chairs—in case word had gotten out and a few extra little ones showed up—plus the slightly bigger one on which she would sit. "So far, so good, Baby Rose." Flo took pride in being prepared.

Those who heard about Flo's project donated books, toys, crayons, paper and a few bits of unused costumes (only the clean ones please) and accessories. Flo's gift was well received. It was fun for her too and she felt appreciated. There was little time between the end of class and curtain call. To make better use of her time, Flo began wearing her clown face to class, knowing she'd have time for small repairs and finishing touches. The children loved it so that Flo decided to incorporate clown face lessons into the learning. Flo told her students about the types of clown faces in circuses—Auguste, Tramp, why she chose an Asian-inspired Whiteface, ways of properly applying stage makeup and more. Flo often brought a few mirrors and her personal makeup case, guiding the children to choose from the numerous creamy tubes and treasures inside so they could create their own faces.

Early on, Flo noticed that several of the children conversed only in their parents' native language, German. Because she grew up speaking and understanding Yiddish—much of it derived from German, Flo was able to communicate with the children and helped them learn English. It was a tribute to her beloved Mama, who spoke mainly Yiddish. This too made Flo happy and proud. Flo's school was meant as a gift for others but was something that forever touched her own heart. Before the next five Ringling seasons ended, Flo had enriched the young lives of more than 25 students.

Flo delighted young and old

1968: Riding High

Flo's performances in the center ring were huge hits. By 1968, she began producing spellbinding acts for herself and other clowns. The spectacular costumes, props, choreography, comedy and staging of Flo's acts proved that she was more than a star performer and Ringling management paid her extra for adding producing to her circus contributions.

Celebrating with a bottle of French bubbly after a sold-out Sunday matinee in Baton Rouge, Miles White learned that one of Flo's favorite performers was Mae West. Flo gushed, "Mae is magnificently stylish—and *oh* so naughty!" Miles thought up a challenge for Flo on the spot. He massaged her ego as he refilled her flute. "YOU my dear, have magnificent style, and timing, and I, for one, know intimately just how naughty you can be!" They both tittered knowingly.

Flo was intrigued and suspicious of where Miles was going with this talk, thinking, "He is charming, but such a prankster." Miles continued. "This will be better than when we snuck you on top of the Spec's payoff float for the '56 Coronation of Mother Goose!" A bit tipsy,

Flo inelegantly snorted, remembering what a hoot that was. She was hooked. "I'll design for you the slinkiest, most elegant Mae West costume fit for Mae West herself! With you in it, your Mae West will outdo the real Mae West!"

Flo started working on the act the next morning. Full of double entendre, the gag's setting placed Mae West in the West. "Mae West and the Stagecoach Incident" became one of the most popular clown acts ever. And as Miles White accurately predicted, Flo out-Mae'd Mae West.

Of all the extravagant costumes Miles White designed for Flo over the years, this was the most elaborate and by far, the slinkiest. For Flo, more pear-shaped than hourglass, who regularly had to pour herself into Miles' most devilishly stunning costumes, this effort was worth having to deny

Flo in Miles White's "Mae West" costume

herself those few Baby Ruth chocolate bars she kept stashed in her trunk.

The highlight of the act came after the stagecoach had entered the ring, pulled by a team of live horses, and abruptly stopped by the outlaw Blinko, Flo's dear friend Ernie Burch. Brandishing a tiny pistol, Blinko held up the stagecoach. He flung open the door and in a state of high drama, Mae West wedged herself from the stagecoach, careful not to muss her wig or large picture hat, while dragging a bustle resembling a large stalk of carrots.

The gag had been going perfectly until the Cincinnati stand. As the roustabouts were preparing for the opening show, they failed to secure the hitch connecting the horses to the stagecoach. That evening, making the turn around the track before arriving at the center ring, the coach rolled over and the horses dragged it upside down for a considerable distance before rescuers were able to slow the horses, stop the coach and come to Flo's aid. Upon being safely extracted from the wreck, Flo, panicked and in a state of general disarray—hat and wig askew, carrots awry, remembered there was an audience surrounding her. She composed herself, stopped and curtsied to her fans before being helped, smiling, waving and hobbling beyond the wild applause of the audience and fellow performers alike. Safely out of earshot of the spotlight, Flo turned to Pat Valdo and began screaming…but politely so, and in character, "Mr. Valdo, Mr. Valdo! I shall henceforth make my entrance on foot!"

Flo charmed snakes and fans alike

CHAPTER 12

1969–1974: Center Rings & Full Circles

At the intersection of her well-established celebrity and global upheaval, Flo's world collided with a new one.

In 1969, she reluctantly ended her 20 year run with Ringling. Several friends, older than she, were retiring. But age wasn't the only factor in their decision. New management was bringing in fresh, younger acts eager to flee from "Behind the Iron Curtain" and the oppressive Communist regimes in Eastern Europe. The talented new performers were willing to accept the low wages; wages which often bested those of Ringling's old timers.

In addition to money, Jackie LeClaire disclosed the more disturbing issue that caused he, Flo and others to leave Ringling. "When the Iron Curtain performers came, they were a pretty repressed group, and closeted in their sexuality. We lost some of our freedom. And it's important to remember too, we weren't far removed from the Holocaust; some of the Eastern Europeans still thought poorly of Jews and homosexuals."

Flo knew what she wanted to do next and wisely, but reluctantly took some time off—a gift she rarely allowed herself. Rested and refreshed after a month, she formed the Albert White Trio, an act she produced and performed with veteran clown friends Kenny Dodd and Billy McCabe.

The enterprise was successful and by mid-1970 the Albert White Trio was in demand. From then on, Flo, Kenny and Billy had the luxury of cherry-picking all the tours they booked. With Kenny or Billy at the wheel of Flo's 1948 aqua Studebaker, they drove Miss Flo—and themselves to the gigs.

Left to right: Billy McCabe, Kenny Dodd and Flo

Although Flo hadn't driven in years, she remained the owner of her cherished vehicle she'd bought during her time at La Tosca. The new Earl Scheib body shop franchise had just opened, and she had them paint the car the color closest to her Turquoise Trailer.

The three friends often drove to Canada to perform with Dobridge International Exhibitions when they weren't touring the U.S., mainly with the Clyde Beatty-Cole Brothers Circus.

In the spring of 1974, Kenny and Flo traveled by air to Hawaii to perform with a unit of the Dobridge show. Shortly after returning to Sarasota, Kenny left to visit family in his native Virginia for the summer.

He and Flo next saw one another in the fall in Daytona where Flo had gone to help another friend, Jimmy Douglas, create wardrobe and develop production "specs" for a show Douglas would be producing. "Flo was enjoying the October sunshine in Jimmy's backyard, sewing, and building props. Even then, Flo was immaculately dressed and groomed, wearing a marvelous yellow sweater," recalled Kenny.

A few weeks after returning home to Sarasota from the Daytona trip, Flo fell ill. It was cancer, a disease which Flo's biological family was and remains predisposed. Mercifully, her battle was brief. She worked as long as she could—through mid-October when she was hospitalized. In November 1974, Flo succumbed to the illness. It had been less than a month since her diagnosis.

As dictated by Jewish custom, Flo was buried two days after she died, returning to the city of her birth, Baltimore. Flo lies between her Mama Ida and Grandfather Abrah in the Meyrowitz family plot at the nation's

Coming full circle, Flo returned as Abraham to Baltimore where she rests among her Meyrowitz family

first Hebrew burial grounds. Mikro Kodesh Beth Israel Hebrew Cemetery is a stone's throw from the Locust Point Docks where Flo's father and grandfather first touched American soil, the first in the family to do so.

With only something of her heritage and given name quietly reclaimed—Abraham Isadore Meyrowitz, Flo's modest headstone hints at nothing of her remarkable life; of those who loved her, of those she loved and the multitudes she delighted along the way and since.

In remembering Flo, Jackie LeClaire spoke for many. "Flo was always, always, always a lady. She would have been a lot more competition for most women had she been born a woman because she was far lovelier than most and had a great personality. She was exhilarating when she walked into a room—lit it way up! She loved to kid, and she loved to laugh. We all loved to make her laugh. She had such a hearty laugh! Flo made everybody look good, because she was so good herself. No one cared who you were kissing or loving, as long as you were good for the show. Flo deserved every ounce of attention and respect she received in circus society. Perhaps she wouldn't have gotten that on the outside. A gay man, or in Flo's case, a woman in a man's body, in regular society? No. That was a very different world. Here, in circus, it was professional ability that counted most and she had that in spades. Flo transformed the ordinary into the extraordinary—most especially herself."

EPILOGUE

Leaving Baltimore with Christian and the C. R. Lamont Wagon Circus, young Abraham stepped through a looking glass to a new life. On the other side was a different name, new family and a person reborn.

In that strange, new world, where chains were meant to secure only tent poles and secrets were irrelevant, Abraham could finally begin to embrace life.

On that fateful Baltimore May day in 1920, Abraham Isadore Meyrowitz ceased to exist and in time became Flo.

She embraced her new life in six welcoming circus families, performing for millions of delighted fans. In later years, Flo was comforted by joyful reunions with Mama Ida and her sisters, and eventually her brothers.

Flo's wildest dreams of fame came true. She became a member of the Ringling clown-elite from 1949 to 1969 performing in extravagant, and decidedly feminine costumes in the U.S., Canada, Mexico and Cuba. In 1952, she appeared in many scenes in Cecil B. DeMille's Oscar-winning Best Picture *The Greatest Show on Earth!* and was leading lady Martha Reye's double in Billy Rose's *Jumbo*. Appearing on the cover of the March 14, 1965 *Baltimore Sun Sunday Magazine,* Flo was the subject of that edition's five page spread, a pictorial feature entitled "A Baltimore Boy Who Ran Off to the Circus."

Flo became known and respected the world over for her meticulously applied Asian-inspired makeup, hand-crafted millinery, miles of shimmering fabrics transformed into dazzling costumes placed just so over undergarments and petticoats that provided umbrage for colossal breasts and bottom. Underneath all of that frippery, there beat a heart of pure gold.

Inside and out of her delicately beaded size 11 slippers,

Courtesy, The Baltimore Sunpapers

worn under her size 15 clown shoes, Flo inspired me to walk the artist path she tread. My cousin David Cohen and I used to pay the highest of compliments to one another by saying "you were born with the Uncle Albert" gene. David, Flo's nephew, was an accomplished dancer, actor and musician. I'm told I emerged into the world singing and dancing. I've studied music and theatre, played and performed on numerous stages, created artworks in many mediums—paintings, clay, glass, and photography, and still enjoy doing so. The writing muscle exercised daily throughout my 30-year communications career, the gifts from extraordinary mentors, a life imbued with rich experiences have all well prepared me for this second career in the literary arts with stories aplenty yet to pen. It may be that having my Uncle in my life for years was enough inspiration for a lifetime. Still, I hope David was right, and I did inherit the "Uncle Albert" gene. Either way, thank you Flo. I trust I've honored your memory with this rendering of your singular, extraordinary story.

Flo was an unusually gifted, giving and gentle soul who courageously replaced rejection and pain with beauty and light.

Her life was pure art.

Flo's life was pure art

*"My Uncle Albert inspired me to
walk the artist's path,"* Deb Carson

ACKNOWLEDGMENTS

My first cousin David Cohen (*ave shalom*, rest in peace) and I often revisited which one of our family members had been born with the "Uncle Albert" gene. As a dancer, actor and musician, David had that gift in spades. Make no mistake, there is a great deal of talent throughout our gene pool—artists, musicians, writers, actors, dancers—but no one has yet fashioned a successful career from such gifts. Uncle Albert—Flo, surely did.

This ten year labor of love could not have been completed on my own. I have many to thank for their encouragement, help, time, and love; sadly, so many more than space allows me to mention here. To you, I offer my deepest apologies, and to all, my abiding gratitude.

For my academic family/friends, I am grateful to my professors, advisors and fellow Florida Studies grad students at the University of South Florida St. Petersburg and Eckerd College. I am indebted to Gary Mormino who encouraged me to write Flo's story as my thesis; had it not been for Gary, Flo's story might have remained only in my heart.

To Jerry Notaro—I hold sacrosanct the dear friendship borne out of your devoted, indefatigable enthusiasm, commitment, candor, knowledge and sage wisdom you've so generously given from thesis to book, to my book presentation/performance of The FLO Show.

To those in the circus community who loved and worked with Flo, and continue to celebrate her legacy, I thank you as well as the Ringling Circus Museum. Had it not been for you—Flo's circus family, this story would have been a slim read indeed. Chief among such beautiful people are Kenny Dodd, and most especially, Jackie LeClaire, whom I first met when I was ten.

Flo's story sparkles because of Jackie. The world lost a world-class showman, masterful storyteller and sweetheart when Jackie went to light up heaven in 2018.

Thank you to my friends who are accomplished writers and artists for coffee talk, support and advice, especially Maria Emilia Faedo, Suzanna Molino Singleton and Jim Schnur.

Jackie LeClaire & Author

To my insightful editor, talented writer, collaborator and La Playa Sister, Nanette Wiser, you made all the difference, and continue doing so every day. You are an incredible talent, stalwart champion and amazing friend who visualized FLO as a film and performance.

Thank you to my family for generously sharing your memories and stories of Flo. No matter how many times I asked questions, you all ceaselessly cheerleaded the project especially my cousins—David Cohen, Fran Cohen Heinith, Leslie Platt Cassale and Jo-Ann Carson Middleman. This labor of love honors all of you. A huge hug to my mother, Marcia Amelia Kallins Carson who loves and supports me no matter what and to my devoted sister Susan Carson Truesdell Dunaway—you both informed Flo's story immeasurably, lending joy and light to the work—as you do always for me.

To my little furry muse Tee and most especially to my talented husband Rocky (the real writer in the family), you hold my heart. Thank you for believing in FLO…and me.

Tee

ABOUT THE AUTHOR - Deb Carson

My mother said from the moment I came into this world, I was singing and dancing. My first love was always the arts. Entering college as a voice major, switching to musical theatre, moving to oral interpretation of poetry/prose/drama, and ultimately recognizing the overwhelming gifts of others with whom I competed, my studies and career trajectory pivoted to marketing communications where I've enjoyed a successful and satisfying career for more than 30 years.

Still, my interest in the arts grew and further developed—writing, singing and playing multiple instruments; adding painting, clay, glass, photography along the way. During the last decade, I've pursued writing as a second career, and wrote FLO first as a film treatment, then for my master's thesis and finally as an unabridged 175-page manuscript which became this book.

Born and raised in Baltimore, I've lived and worked in Boston, Washington, D.C., Norfolk and as an adult chose Florida for my permanent home in 1991. As a child, I had visited with my family to see Flo, my grandparents and other relatives in the Sarasota area. I loved the Gulf of Mexico as did Flo. I have lived in Sarasota, Sebring, Cape Coral, Jacksonville, and now St. Petersburg. My experiences in all these places provides a rich tapestry that never ceases to inspire me and inform my work.

BOOKINGS

Carson performs the multimedia companion piece to this book, "The FLO Show," developed in collaboration with creative partner Nanette Wiser. Audiences have proclaimed it a "colorful, lively, joyful and emotion-packed presentation."

To book an appearance, or subscribe to receive updates, visit www.DebCarsonWrites.com.

Follow Deb Carson on Facebook (https://www.facebook.com/debbie.carson.58) and LinkedIn (https://www.linkedin.com/in/deb-carson-2b2bb66/).